JUMLA

A NURSE'S STORY

Radha Paudel

nepa~laya

Published by

publication nepa~laya
Kathmandu, Nepal
Phone: +977-1-4439786
email: publication@nepalaya.com.np
www.nepalaya.com.np

© **Radha Paudel**

The moral rights of the author has been asserted.
First edition 2016
1

Translated by : Dev Paudel & Ishan Gurung

Cover Design : INCS

Cover Image : Mohan Mainali
(Ruins in Khalanga after the Maoist attack)

Printed and bound in Nepal by
Jagadamba Press, Hattiban, Lalitpur

ISBN - 978-9937-9090-3-7

JUMLA: A Nurse's Story a memoir by Radha Paudel

A Few Words

I am a nurse. I don't understand the politics behind conflict. I just see the wounds that conflict leaves. After witnessing the attack on Khalanga, this is my attempt to heal those wounds and the scars that have been left behind.

After leaving a government job and starting developmental work, I became well acquainted with the poverty, social injustice and conflict affecting the Karnali people. Since I had also experienced poverty in my childhood, I had empathy for their suffering. I saw the terror of war close up and experienced the pressure of having to work caught between the Maoist rebels and the security forces. The biggest thing, however, was that I understood the state of mind of the people of Karnali, who didn't even hope of dreaming for a better future. I felt this experience should be recorded.

I would like to thank everyone who has helped me to come this far. These include the friends of "Miteri Village - Let's Live Together" of Action Works Nepal; Saroj Dahal and Uttam Blon Lama who encouraged me to publish this book; Narayan Niraula who typed the text; nepa~laya who took care of publishing; as well as my brothers-in-law Umakanta Regmi, Thakur Prasad Wasti, and Lila Raj Bhandari. I would also like to thank my sons and daughters Anupa, Sarupa, Anil, Sanjeev, Sanjita, Saurav, Sharmila, Mamata, Alisha, Alina, Laxmikanta and Sahansheela, my brothers-in-law Subash and Bharat, and my granddaughters Samriddhi and Prashidi.

My thanks also goes to Sudeep Shrestha who edited the original book in Nepali, Dev Paudel and Ishan Gurung for the English translation and Dr. Edmund Kellerman for editing it. I also express my gratitude to Linda Trigg and Keshav P. Koirala for further editing and fine-tuning.

Radha Paudel
Khalanga, Jumla

All known and unknown people who lost their lives in the Khalanga attack and those who still lose their lives every day due to poverty, social inequality and injustice.

CONTENTS

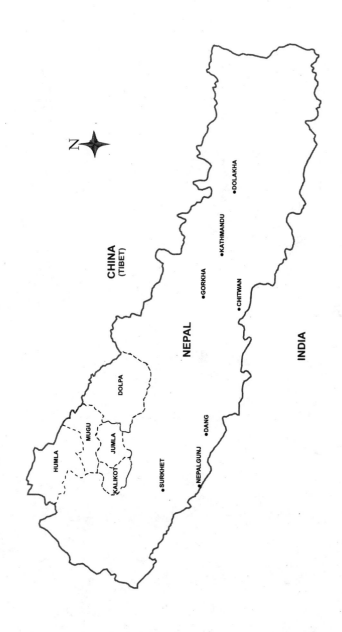

THE BEGINNING...

An outbreak of diarrhoea in Jumla was as common as the spread of common cold in Kathmandu. But something unusual happened that year.

In mid-February, the number of patients with diarrhoea coming for treatment at the Jumla hospital started to increase. Usually an increase in cases was seen later, around the months of May and June, when people began eating the new crops of wheat and barley.

Jumlis were worried by this early onslaught of diarrhoea, maybe for the first time in their memories. Meetings and discussions about it were held in the District Administration Office (DAO), also probably for the first time.

Earlier, on 14 November 2002, the Maoist rebels had brutally attacked Jumla's district headquarters, Khalanga. Most of the government officers there had been appointed since the attack. They had to meet and submit monthly reports to the DAO on the third of each month and the DAO would issue orders accordingly. The telephone towers had been destroyed so there was no system of quick communication. Post was the only alternative or we had to send someone reliable to convey a message in person.

The outbreak of diarrhoea was the first item on the agenda of the regular meeting on 15 February. Reasons were sought, suspicions were raised and one conclusion was reached.

There was a rumour that the dead bodies of the Maoists killed in the November assault might have been thrown into the Tila River. The scorching heat of the sun might have started decomposing the bodies. This same river was the only source of drinking water for the villagers. Contamination of water seemed the only viable cause for the untimely outbreak of diarrhoea.

"If that's the case, this is a serious problem," people said, "What should we do?"

The DAO issued a decree immediately that the river was to be inspected and any corpses removed.

7 March

It was International Women's Day but the DAO had decided that would be the day to clean the river.

Primary responsibility for organising the celebration of International Women's Day in Jumla rested with the Women's Development Branch where I worked. We had some events planned for the day.

In the meeting, I expressed my concerns to the Central District Officer, Krishnashyam Budhathoki.

"7 March is International Women's Day," I said.

"So what?" Budhathoki replied.

"The Women's Development Office has worked out a programme," I said, "There's no way we can undo it. Can't we inspect the river some other day?"

"Then you don't have to come," he said dismissively. "You don't have to be involved."

I was very disappointed to hear this.

"I want to take part, Sir," I said. "That's the only day I can't make it. I'm available any other day."

"No, Radha," he continued, "We will do it that day. It's Saturday, so we can work without interruption."

The office heads and other employees supported his idea.

I tried to raise my voice again but they didn't want to listen to me and started talking among themselves.

I was alone in the meeting and very disappointed. But still, I kept quiet.

There was a reason they were trying to exclude me from the process of cleaning the river. It was because removing the dead bodies was regarded as "risky." It wasn't risky because of the threat of disease or because the task was particularly difficult but because of the traditional belief that where there are dead bodies, there are also ghosts. Even in cities, educated people only go to such places under extreme pressure. What to say about the more backward people in Jumla? Maybe they wanted to take only the bravest people to clean the river just in case the ghosts came?

But are only men brave? Is that written anywhere in holy scripture?

I was aware that some of my male colleagues were afraid to go to the river, though they wouldn't say anything publicly for fear of being called cowards. But I really wanted to go, not to show that I was braver than the men but because I believed it was my duty as a health worker to be involved in an important undertaking related to public health. Moreover, villagers were telling mysterious stories about the scattered corpses and I wanted to learn the truth for myself.

But how could I abandon the International Women's Day celebration after all the preparations we had made?

My heart grew heavy.

If I went with the men, then I was afraid the programme to celebrate International Women's' Day might not be very good. And what would I do if male friends started to gloat because of that? On the other hand, if I didn't go I was detaching myself from an important undertaking affecting the whole district.

I was in a quandary.

I shared my dilemma with the acting Women's Development Officer, Uma Karki. "We're here," she said "Don't worry about the programme. We can handle it."

I advised her on what to do and how to do it. "Please start the programme," I said, "I'll come as soon as I can."

My heart felt a little lighter.

That morning we gathered at the DAO. The heads of all the offices in the district were there.

We travelled across the airport to Dangsanghu where we divided into two groups to search each side of the river. We agreed to inspect the river and, if any dead bodies of either humans or animals were found, they were to be buried in deep holes.

As I had to leave early to return for the International Women's Day celebration, I didn't cross to the far side of the river.

Even though mid-March was approaching, the water in the Tila River was cold. It was, however, becoming a lot shallower. We started working our way down the river, stepping on and jumping over big rocks along the way. If we had just been there for sight-seeing, it would have been lovely. But our purpose was very different. Many people in my group began to drag their feet. Some were petrified and walked very slowly. I, on the other side, was not afraid at all and was leading the group.

As I moved forward, my thoughts went back to the terrible attack four months earlier and I started to feel like I was reliving the experience. I didn't hear the raging water or the chirping of the birds. My ears were full of the sounds of gunfire and the cries of people coming from all directions.

We hadn't even walked for five minutes along the river bank when we started to see numerous big holes which had clearly been created by human hands. There were bones scattered widely around the holes. We felt as if all the wood in the area was not wood at all but the remains of dead people. Some bones looked normal while others had been blackened due to exposure to the weather. Dogs had scattered some bones as well.

I had heard rumours that the Maoists had dug holes on the banks of the river and buried the bodies of their dead so the security forces wouldn't find them and that seemed to be true. I was exploring these holes, clearing the soil with my own hands.

"Look! There's a complete body over here," one of my companions called out.

Most of us ran towards him, although some people didn't go, afraid of what they might see. I had a small stick in my hand and I used it to start digging the soil away. The body was that of a male less than 25 years of age wearing a blue tracksuit and brown shoes.

The body was papery-white. His eyes were closed and thin skin was attached to his bones. I saw small holes in his chest and head, probably the result of being shot. I had heard that fish ate the fingers of people who drowned in rivers but I didn't see anything like that here. The body was just not breathing. Otherwise, he looked like he could wake up at any moment.

Feeling sad, I had taken just a few more steps when I saw an even more devastating sight. Small fragments of human bodies were scattered all over the ground as if a clay doll had been dropped from a great height and shattered. We couldn't tell which part of the human body these pieces belonged to.

Some people couldn't stand to look and were spitting just like after chewing tobacco. The scene didn't affect me that much, however, because I had seen horrible and frightening things when I worked as an anaesthetic assistant in the operating theatre. We even used to drink tea to refresh ourselves during long operations. My companions were amazed at my reaction. I was becoming more sympathetic and compassionate and felt pity for the dead rather than fear or disgust.

By noon we had walked along the river as far as the Agriculture Development Office. Some people in our group started to dig deep trenches to bury the bodies and scattered body parts but I had to leave that work to get back to the DAO for the International Women's Day celebration.

Later that evening I learned what had transpired by the river after I left. My colleagues had found another four complete dead bodies.

Whose sons were they? Whose husbands were they? Whose fathers were they? There were no answers to these questions although their bodies had rested on the banks of the Tila River for the past four months. For the shooter, it was just another shot and their comrades hadn't even tried to save them. How cheap had life become? Probably nobody even cared if they were alive or dead. Hold a wounded friend in your arms but then leave him on a river bank and move on? A quick death would have been more humane but imagine the ordeal these people had gone through had they lived for a couple of days. Imagine how they would have called for help with their throats parched and how hopeless they must have felt when nobody answered. How many days must they have cried alone, thinking about their families?

We hadn't realised for four months that their tears had mixed with the waters of the Tila River.

There were so many other tears we haven't seen.

1

FATHER, HOW POOR ARE WE?

I was well aware of the fact that we were poor but I had no way of knowing how poor we really were. I used to say to my father, "Father, we're poor, right?" and he would reply "No, my dear, there are people poorer than us living in Jumla."

Seriously? Poorer than us!

I was surprised.

"Father, don't they even have anything to eat or any clothes to wear?"

"Not enough."

I was astounded.

"Can't they go to school?"

"Most of them can't."

"And do they also have to live in the dark, without electricity, like us?"

Father remained silent for some time. I stared at him, waiting for an answer.

"They live in greater darkness than us," said Father, "You have to study hard and then, after your studies are finished, serve the poor in Jumla."

I was exalted.

All children believe their father is the most intelligent man in the world. I felt the same.

When he spoke, my father could charm the birds out of the trees. He used to delight us children with his stories, always ending on just the right note. I never thought of him as just a milkman. I held him in much higher regard.

Father was a connoisseur, especially when it came to cooking and eating. There was magic in his hands, not just in his words. I used to wait eagerly for the four days when my mother would have her period and all responsibility in the kitchen fell to my father. He cooked very enthusiastically and I loved his food. I used to make fun of my mother, "You should always have your period, Mother. The food Father cooks is better than yours."

Mother would give me a scornful look.

It used to be terrible when Mother got sick. My heart wanted my mother to get well soon. Poor Mother! But my stomach didn't agree with my heart. The longer Mother's sickness went on, the more I would be eating the delicious food made by my father. It was a predicament.

Later, I found out my father used to be a domestic helper. I heard it from my mother one day during a discussion at home about who was the better cook.

I was extremely happy that day, truly happy. Anybody could have a father who was an official. But could anyone have a father who was a cook? None of my friends' fathers were cooks. When their mothers had their periods, they had to do the cooking at home. I, on the other hand, didn't have to.

I had not seen anybody's father who was as awesome as mine.

There was a long story behind Father being a cook.

Our ancestral home was in Sahinlitar, Lamjung. Mother's parents' home was also there. My father doesn't have many memories of his parents because they passed away when he was young. Then his aunt took care of him and my father lived in Gorkha, his mother's home town, for a few years. Those times were hard. He didn't get enough food to eat. Instead, he had to work in the fields, weeding, planting rice and doing other farming jobs. His aunt had even less food than he did so Father would steal maize, soybeans and rice to share with his aunt. They used to cook and eat together.

One day, my father got bored with the life he was living. He was done with it. Why, he never said. When I heard this story, I didn't understand why someone would be fed up with his life so I didn't bother to ask the reason. Anyway, he left his home and reached Jhapa. Looking back on it now, I realise he must have fled at that time because of too much work and too little food. He started to help in the zonal administrator's office. He was a connoisseur of good food and so it was there that my father became a cook.

Later, he moved to Gauriganj of Bharatpur in Chitwan where he started farming and selling milk.

And there I was born in 1973.

My parents both felt that learning was only accomplished by reading out aloud.

That's why I read my lessons aloud, just as if I were reading from the Swosthani, a religious text. Father used to recline on his bed nearby and listen to me with a smile on his face. Mother used to sit on the floor and watch me as I memorised my texts.

I have five siblings, four sisters and a brother. I am the second youngest daughter. All of us read together. Because there was a good atmosphere in my house, a few friends from the village also came to our home to study after dinner. With so many people gathered there, it used to be difficult for us to find a place to sit. There were no chairs or desks. And no separate rooms either.

I wanted my father to buy me a new pair of shoes but he didn't have the money. He put me on his bicycle and took me to the bazaar, telling me stories all the way there. And then he brought me back home without buying any shoes. I had been so mesmerised by his words that I completely forgot about the shoes. I felt that even the teachers in my school didn't speak as eloquently as my father. He never scolded us when we made mistakes but made us see the error of our ways by telling relevant stories with a moral.

I had never seen such a good father.

I heard him speak to other people in the same way. He was so immensely knowledgeable that I wondered if he might also be a school teacher. But he never came to teach at my school and I never saw him go to any other school. I never heard other students call him "Devi Prasad Sir" or saw them leaving him with loads of homework. He must not be a teacher, I decided, otherwise he would come home with chalk dust on his hands and clothes.

Then he must be a government official, I thought, a high ranking one.

But, in fact, my father used to sell milk. He used to milk the buffaloes early in the morning and take the milk to sell in town. In the evening, he used to buy rice and bring it back in the milk can. I used to take care of his accounts although he could do calculations in his head.

We stayed in a newly constructed house. It had two storeys and a thatched roof.

There was no electricity in our house. We used to make *tuki*, a type of home-made lamp. For this, we used to collect my mother's empty medicine bottles. We made a wick out of threads and inserted it into a bottle. Then we added kerosene and lit the tuki. We gathered around the *tuki* to study, like insects gathered around a flame.

When I read aloud, I used to sway back and forth. "She doesn't need a swing. Just put a book in front of her and she starts to swing by herself," my mother said.

Father laughed and I went red with embarrassment. I could control my swaying for some time but eventually I would fall back into the habit as if my body were in tune with the words coming out of my mouth.

After finishing my studies for the evening, I used to sleep next to my father on a small bed. Mother used to sleep on the floor on the western side of the room. My brother and younger sister slept with her. My elder sisters slept on the other side of the room. I used to put one hand under my father's head and with the other hand play with his earlobe.

I couldn't fall sleep without talking with Father for 10 or 15 minutes.

"Father, I don't have a good notebook and pencil."

"So what?" Father used to say, caressing my hair with his eyes closed.

"What do you mean 'so what'? My friends will make fun of me." I pinched his earlobe.

"Aah!" he said and pulled my hair softly. I giggled.

"Father, when will we be rich?" I asked.

He used to bring up the story of Jumla.

"We are rich, my dear, richer than the people of Jumla."

"How are the people of Jumla?" I got excited.

In a sweet voice, Father told me about his memories of Jumla, including its poverty.

"I stayed in Jumla for seven months when I went there with my supervisor in 1960."

"When was that, Father?"

"That was a long time ago, my child. You weren't even born yet.

"Was Mother born?"

"Mother wasn't here either."

I was astounded.

"I wasn't married to her at the time, dumb-head," he laughed.

13

I got angry and pinched his earlobe so he pulled my hair again.

"Do you want to hear the rest of the story or not?"

"Yes, I want to hear it," I mumbled and kept quiet.

My father met a lot of people in Jumla in those seven months. They all lived in hardship. They didn't have enough food to eat or clothes to wear. Education was a far-fetched story. He found the women there to be in the most miserable situation. Their clothes were filthy and the skin on their hands was worn due to dirt.

One day when he met some of the women at the river, he gave them a bar of soap. At first, they didn't want to use it. But when Father insisted, they used it to clean themselves. How could hands which had not been cleaned for ages be cleaned in one shot? Instead, their skin started to bleed due to abrasion from the bar of soap!

They were so poor that they couldn't even wash themselves.

Every night before cuddling and sleeping next to Father, my child brain used to be disturbed by the thought of poverty-stricken Jumla.

Oh my God! What would it be like to live in Jumla?

I had heard a lot about Jumla from my father. After three years studying as a nurse in Pokhara, I understood the dire situation in remote hill areas like Baglung and Parvat.

After finishing my nursing studies in 1994, I came to Kathmandu to search for a job. For three months, I submitted applications at various places and was eventually selected for the job in Bharatpur Hospital on a temporary contract. I was made permanent within a few months.

I came to Kathmandu again in 1994 for a three month training programme organised by the World Health Organization (WHO). This training programme boosted my confidence a lot and had a significant impact on my life. Only four people were selected for that programme and I was one of them. I didn't even know how to use a computer at the time. Much of what I am today, both personally and professionally, I owe to that training.

Everyone says you won't understand Nepal by staying in Kathmandu. The way I look at it, Kathmandu is like a laboratory in which health professionals can study all the ailments which can be found throughout the nation. It's a hub where one meets patients from all over the country: diarrhoea patients from Jajarkot, encephalitis patients from Sarlahi, patients with cancer, patients with AIDS, people injured in accidents and women with uterine prolapse. From talking to these patients we learned about the miserable state of the health services throughout the country. In terms of refining our skills as health professionals and preparing us for any challenges which might come our way while working alone in remote areas with limited resources, I believe the experience of working in Kathmandu was invaluable.

I honed my skills every day.

There are two methods of learning – by doing and by seeing. I got the opportunity to do both. I was born and raised in poverty so I learned about that through my own experience. Then, during my four years working with patients in Bharatpur Hospital, I learned about hardship by seeing the experiences of others.

The human body is a precious gift from the God but,

whenever I heard patients wailing, I also thought the body could be a source of tremendous suffering. The job of a nurse involved consistently seeing the suffering of others, empathising with their pain and trying to find ways to ease it, which was far more than a doctor had to deal with.

I treated countless patients in Bharatpur Hospital. Among those, there were three cases in particular that touched my soul.

The first case involved a seven-year-old girl.

She had been raped by her own cousin, aged 18. When I think of her, I still cry even today. Her uterus and bladder had been badly torn. There were wounds all over her body. There was no anaesthesiologist, so I had to sedate her myself before the operation, which was carried out by a general surgeon because there were no gynaecologists available.

To see a rape victim of such a tender age disturbed me enormously. If there could be a case such as that coming from a suburb near to Bharatpur, how terrible the condition of children who become victims of domestic violence in the remote districts must have been? How many kids must have died without even seeing a hospital? These questions struck me like a knife in my heart.

That girl was treated for two months in the hospital before she was discharged. I used to visit her every day before work.

Then there was the case of a 60-year-old woman. I used to visit her before work every day as well.

That lady was from Parvat but had moved to Chitwan. She came to the hospital through my mother. I was astonished to hear about her case. It had been 18 years since she had had a uterine prolapse but she was so ashamed that she didn't tell anyone. She covered the base of a torch light with plastic and used that to hold the uterus in place inside her.

Oh my God! I found it hard to imagine how anyone could have endured that for so long.

To go into detail, the plastic had been in place so long that it had become attached to the internal muscles. It was very difficult to separate the plastic from the muscle and it involved a long operation. The work of an anaesthetic assistant like me is hard during a long operation. I was always afraid the patient would stop breathing.

During that time, the operating theatre in Bharatpur Hospital was also not as up-to-date as it is today. There wasn't even any equipment to measure the amount of oxygen being administered. We had to trust our hands and eyes to make sure the oxygen was flowing. From time to time, I used to insert my hand inside the patient's face-mask to test if they were breathing or not. We had to check the colour of the blood regularly. If the colour was dark red then we had to increase the rate of oxygen flow. We could also check by pressing on the patient's nails. If the colour was red when the nail was pressed and released, then the patient was ok but if the colour was white then we surmised that the heart and lungs were not working properly.

I had learned to assess the condition of patients without all the proper anaesthetic equipment during the WHO training programme.

Thank God, the operation on that old woman was successful. She survived.

However, my heart started to burn. There could be so

many women like her who had hidden their ailments for years. In particular, they were embarrassed to share problems relating to their reproductive health and that embarrassment had no doubt cost many women their lives. But how could talking about health services in big cities ever solve these problems which were hidden away in the villages? For that, we health professionals needed to give up city life and go to the villages to serve, didn't we?

These questions tormented me.

The third case involved a 27-year-old woman from Manang who had lost a lot of blood during labour. Instead of the head coming out first, the child's hands were the first part of its body to emerge from the birth canal. As a result, it was not possible for the rest of the body to come out. The mother had lost consciousness.

The hands of the child were swollen and bluish in colour, looking bloodless. We had given up hope for both the child and the mother. The situation was such that, even if we performed an operation, neither was likely to survive, however, without the operation there was no chance either could live.

We decided to give it a try.

We performed the operation and took the child out. It was already dead. The mother was still unconscious. There was very little blood in her body: her haemoglobin level was just two grams when normally there has to be nine grams in order to perform an operation. The incision in the mother did not start healing because of the lack of blood. Her abdomen was wide open and we could see her intestines and uterus inside. After receiving more than eight pints of blood within the course of two weeks, her wound started healing and she survived.

Oh my God! Women are in such a sorry state!

That woman was from a well-off family. They knew that taking her to the hospital could save her life, so she was brought from Manang to Bharatpur. How many other mothers must have died during pregnancy, not being able to safely give birth? How many children had never even seen the light of day because of unsafe deliveries?

Many health professionals locate themselves in cities. No one wants to go to remote villages. Many are just interested in earning money to at least pay back what was invested in their education to become a doctor or nurse. Providing health services has become a business. The financial investment in getting a degree needs to be recouped as quickly as possible. With attitudes such as that, who would go to the villages? Are health services only for cities? People living in remote villagers don't have access to electricity, roads or education. They are also deprived of health care. Should people in these villages have to die just because they had no access to simple medicines like paracetamol?

I was trapped in a suffocating web of questions.

Being close to my patients and empathising with their pain and sorrow made me a more confident nurse. And a better person as well.

I stopped saying to my father, "We're poor, right?" because I had realised there were many people who were more poor and disadvantaged than we were. My horizons and my way of looking at life and the world were getting broader. During that time, I decided I would live in the community and do community work. I felt that just treating disease alone was not providing a true health service. It was the responsibility of health professionals to help people think rationally and remove superstitions, as well as dealing with diseases at the grassroots level. My presence or absence would make no difference in a city, whereas a village needed me. I decided I would go to Jumla, the Jumla of my father's stories, after I finished my studies.

My father had planted the seed of Jumla in my mind and during my time working in Bharatpur Hospital that seed grew into a large tree.

I enrolled in a two-year bachelor's degree programme at the Tribhuvan University Teaching Hospital in Maharajganj, Kathmandu. I was in the top four of 10 entrants. My major was Community Health, a subject I chose in preparation for going to Jumla.

During this period, I learned more about the remoteness and the dreadful state of the health services in the Karnali region. Some colleagues from Karnali Technical Institute told shocking stories about Jumla, which my father had never told me.

My forehead started to perspire when I heard about the suffering of the people there. There was a senior sister who had taught at Jumla Technical Institute. She was in my class. Whenever I talked to her, I felt as if I was already in Jumla.

During this time, I completed a Masters in Health Education as well. And at that point, an opportunity came that changed the direction of my life.

I had applied for a position in the Safe Maternity Programme of the UK's Department for International

Development (DFID) and was called for an interview. It must have been a coincidence but the interviewers said, "There are new programmes starting in Jumla and in Nawalparasi. Where would you prefer to go?"

Everyone knows we dream in our sleep. In my experience, whoever day-dreams cannot sleep. I had dreamed about Jumla from my childhood. Father had shown me those dreams. His words – "My daughter will go to Jumla to serve the poor once she finishes her studies" – were always with me. But how could I get there? Where would the offer come from? After so many years of wondering, the dream was coming true.

I thought of my father, remembering the story that he told about the women who had never washed their hands.

For me, it was like a light in the darkness. I replied immediately, "I will go to Jumla."

I was extremely excited to share this news with my father. I was going to serve the poor of Jumla, just as he had always wanted. I thought my father would be overjoyed when he heard the news.

But all of a sudden new thoughts came into my mind. Would my father really be ready to send me off to Jumla? In my father's days, Jumla was peaceful and secure but now it was a stronghold of the Maoist rebels.

Every day there was news of murder and violence there. Would a father, no matter how principled, want to see his daughter going to a far-away place during a time of conflict? In addition to that, I was leaving the permanent job that I had at the Bharatpur Hospital.

I knew my father well. Regardless of what he had said earlier, I became convinced he would never let me go to Jumla. But I also didn't want to leave without telling him where I was going.

I tried to work my going to Jumla into a long and positive story but I was right – my father didn't like the idea. He made it clear that he would prefer me to stay in Bharatpur.

"Leaving a permanent job and going to Jumla?" he said.

As long as I could remember, I had never heard people say good things about Jumla. Adjectives like "poor" and "remote" always came attached to the names of the districts in Karnali like Jumla, Humla, Dolpa, Mugu and Kalikot.

The newspapers also often printed sad stories, sometimes about famine there or people dying of diarrhoeal diseases. Viral influenza was also prevalent. Every year hundreds of people from there were forced to go to India in search of work.

It was not, therefore, surprising that my friends didn't believe at first that I was going to Jumla. After they realised it was true, they started to make fun of me. "Are you going there to make a lot of money?" some joked. Others said, "You won't last long." Many expressed concern about the Maoist insurgency. "With people being killed in Jumla every day, only a lunatic would go there," they said.

I was surprised when I first heard that people in Jumla were poorer than us. We were no longer as poor as we used to be but Jumla was still the same. Why were there so many poverty-stricken people in Jumla? Now I understood.

While even Nepalis treated Jumla as some sort of backward

foreign country, how could it ever develop? How would the livelihood of the people in Jumla ever be improved?

Despite the views of my friends, I had made up my mind.

2001. Rainy season.

The Programme Coordinator said she was going to take me to Jumla with her. "You can go and stay in Surkhet and start learning the work," said she, "Then I'll come and get you and we can go to Jumla together."

However, she was reluctant to even come to Surkhet and I guessed she didn't want to go to Jumla at all. If I had to rely on her, who knew long I would end up waiting in Surkhet? I decided to go to Jumla on my own.

Illiterate people from Nepal had gone to work in countries where they didn't even understand the language. Why did I need someone to escort me within my own country?

Nonetheless, it was very difficult to get flights to Jumla due to bad weather. Furthermore, the airport in Jumla was in the process of being tarmacked so planes were unable to land there. To get a ride on a helicopter was similar to winning the great battle of Mahabharata.

I had the phone number of the owner of the Everest Hotel in Jumla, Sunil Sharma. I called him from Surkhet and he told me a way to use contacts to get a ticket to come on a helicopter. This proved easier than I expected and I got a ticket but my heart was filled with guilt. People had been waiting for more than two weeks just to get a ticket and had started to recognise each other.

"If they see you, they might get angry and pick a fight with you," said the helicopter station manager on the phone. "You keep your bags in our office and pretend you're not going anywhere. I'll tell you when the helicopter's ready."

I became really sad, hearing that. I felt like I was doing an injustice to the passengers who were stranded in the airport because they couldn't get a seat. I regretted getting the ticket by using my contacts.

But what other option did I have? I didn't want to stay in Surkhet. That wasn't my workplace. There were lots of health services in Surkhet. But in Jumla? Jumla really needed me. At least, I felt that way at the time.

Making myself strong, I followed the directions of the station manager and flew towards Jumla in the helicopter.

I was excited.

What would Jumla be like?

The blaring sound of the chopper was hurting my ears.

I had once taken a plane flight from Kathmandu to Bhairahawa but that wasn't as loud as this.

The chopper started to fly like a bird. There were only two passengers, myself and a man. There were lots of parcels and barrels of tar going to Jumla with us. We couldn't see the pilot in front because of the pile of parcels. As we flew, our bodies would sometimes lean towards the left and sometimes lean towards the right. Sometimes we would sit up straight.

Whenever the chopper swerved, it felt as if the barrels of tar might hit us. Flying over the high hills and mountains, I felt as if I were riding on a flying horse like in a story my father used to tell me. I tried to look down through the window. I could see a few huts on the top of the hills and in the gorges. People must be living there. I scrutinised the view. I saw a trail like a thin line. However I couldn't see any schools. Where would the kids from those huts go to school?

I looked to the left and to the right. My mother used to part her hair in the middle. Seeing rivers flowing through the middle of hills reminded me of my mother and almost brought tears to my eyes. In the distance, the view started to get hazy. My eyes felt uncomfortable as if I had dust in them so I blinked and my vision cleared.

The helicopter was circling above Jumla Airport. I was surprised to see a black fence around the airport but, as we flew closer to the ground, the sight became clearer. It wasn't a fence at all but a line of local people standing behind barbed wire. They had come to the airport hoping for work as porters.

As I left the airport, a group of children came towards me. I could see some men and women coming as well. Most of them were old. Some were even disabled. Bending and twisting their arms and legs, and smiling a little, they came towards me.

"We haven't eaten anything. Let us carry your luggage," they said, gesturing towards their bellies.

Before I could even reply, they started to pull at my bags – "I will carry them! I will carry them!" – I was speechless. In the end, I chose two children to carry my bags. Both looked absolutely pathetic. They had sores on their faces due to running noses. The dried mucus between their noses and lips looked like a moustache. They wore black woolen shawls, which were torn and full of holes. How could they offer any protection against the cold of Jumla? Their clothes were also torn and patched in dozens of places and their toes poked out from their broken shoes. Their hair looked like it had never been washed and their faces were dirty and hardened by the cold.

"What are your names?" I asked

Hesitatingly, they told me their names. They were *dalits*. "Don't you go to school?"

As a response they moved their heads to signal "No."

They were speaking the Jumli dialect. I understood but couldn't speak in the same way so I asked my questions in Nepali and they replied in their own language. They had never been outside of Khalanga Bazaar. They were 12-years-old or so but had never seen the inside of a school and had no education at all.

After reaching the hotel, I asked the owner, Goma Sharma, about these boys. She said their fathers had disappeared all of a sudden. Nobody knew if he had been taken by the Maoists or had fled to India or if he was dead or alive. Their mothers had remarried and the boys were eking out a living by working as porters in the cold of Jumla. They were also supporting their grandparents.

All night, I thought about those two boys. Was being an orphan or poor anyone's choice? Didn't those kids want to go to school? Poor children didn't even get the chance to play on their mothers' laps for long.

Tears rolled down my cheeks before I even realised it.

My father and his descriptions of Jumla came to my mind.

Father had come to Jumla in 1960. Born in Lamjung and orphaned at a tender age, he had travelled to Jumla. How did he end up here? It was so remote even now, how would it have been back then? Man goes wherever destiny leads him. Had my father settled here at that time, I could have been like those kids. I was lucky because my father chose the plains of Chitwan and I was born in a much less isolated place than Jumla.

Pondering this, I realised that the birthplace of a person was not their choice. The heart-rending side of Jumla had presented itself to me on the very first day.

I thought about my own childhood. I had walked without shoes. I had gone to bed hungry. I had carried loads larger than myself. I had cut grass and worked in the fields. But I had never been as poor as this.

There were times when I thought I was miserable but now I realised the true meaning of the word.

Father had been telling the truth.

The people in Jumla were much poorer than we were.

Many of my friends from nursing college were in Britain. Once in a while, they emailed me to come to the UK. "Why are you staying in Nepal? Come to Britain. Everything's here."

I wanted to write back, "Is Jumla in Britain?"

I considered myself very fortunate to have the chance to

work in Jumla and not in Britain. Britain could get a lot of nurses like me. But in Jumla, I was the only one. In Britain, my presence wouldn't have been worth a penny while in Jumla it was invaluable.

I worked as a Human Resource Development Officer. In one sense, it was a managerial position. In Nepal, once somebody becomes the chief of an office, he will have a fat belly, a sign of prosperity, and a lady chief will be wearing tons of makeup. Ladies try to avoid going to places like Jumla, of course, and, even if they go, nobody trusts them, especially if they are young. My first challenge was to prove myself and to win the trust of the people.

I started wearing a sari. Usually a sari is worn by married women only. On the way to the office, I also used to put a *tika* on my forehead like a married woman. But still, nobody acknowledged my position. Everybody called me "Sister." For them, I was a nurse who treated patients, not a manager. This made my work a bit difficult at first. Many people tried to obstruct me – and are still doing it today.

But I was not going to give up.

My education played a very big part in my winning people's confidence. Everybody bit their tongues when I told them that I had a Master's degree in Health Education, a Master's degree in Sociology, a Bachelor's degree in Nursing and four years' experience as an anaesthetic assistant. My education became my greatest asset when I started working in Jumla.

Coincidentally, the doctor there, whose last name was the same as mine, had studied with my elder sister, Bindu. Even though everything was generally fine with him, I was disappointed that he was not really interested in Jumla and showed no enthusiasm for working there. He had just come to fulfill the government requirement that he work in a remote place. "We can't achieve anything here, Sister," he said, "Just keep everyone happy while you serve your time here and then move on."

He tried to make me understand in the Jumli dialect, "Work here, get experience, then go."

I just smiled to nullify this negativity.

We didn't have a separate office. Since it was wartime and it was a programme of the Nepali and British governments, we were given a room in the Jumla Hospital.

In the one-room office, there were four plastic chairs, two tables, two chairs with cushions and one cupboard on the wall. That was it. For security reasons, we were advised to live as simply as possible. Therefore, even in the cold of Jumla, there was no heater or carpet. During winter, my hands often felt frozen. I hadn't taken many winter clothes when I moved to Jumla. I didn't know then that thermal coats would keep me warm and, even had I known, I didn't have enough money to buy one. But I looked at the way others were faring. They were getting by with even thinner clothes than mine. I thought, we are all surviving and the feeling of being cold would just go away.

Our room had a new wire mesh door. It was a little stiff and squeaked whenever it was opened or closed. One day, a lady came through the door in a rush and said in a single breath: "Sister, sister, there is a lady suffering from diarrhoea.

Please come quickly."

Her name was Tara Nepali. Her husband was in the police force. She had started living back in her parents' home with her son after her husband had married another woman. She helped in the Hospital Development Committee on a salary of Rs 1000 per month. And that was after an increase. She was a very honest person and never said "No" to any work. Perhaps that was because her job wasn't permanent yet or maybe it was due to the economic difficulties she was experiencing after her husband left.

Tara was the only female helper in the Jumla Hospital. She had a cheerful face and was a little timid. If she saw patients with serious problems, she would sometimes be very afraid. She worked from early in the morning till late at night. She didn't stamp her foot out of anger, even if she had to stay late. She didn't pull faces. I hadn't worked with anyone as helpful as Tara. Many other helpers didn't care about time, got drunk and fell asleep in the office, or they quarrelled or made excuses to avoid work. Some just wanted to gossip. But Tara didn't have those bad qualities.

Tara had come to see me that day after finding the patient with diarrhoea in a serious condition. I immediately wanted to rush out with her and go to the patient but I stopped myself.

I hadn't come to Jumla as a nursing sister and didn't have permission to treat patients there. I realised that if I started treating patients just because of an emotional reaction on my part, then I would have to continue doing it. Admittedly, not many patients came to the Jumla Hospital but, even so, I didn't want to take on the responsibility which rightly belonged to the doctors and nurses there.

"Why should I come if it's just a case of diarrhoea?" I said, "Call whoever has been treating the patient."

Tara was standing in the doorway, holding it open with one hand. One of her legs was inside and the other was outside. She said in a tearful voice, "*Gali gali*, sister, the patient is serious." In Jumla, if you want to plead for something, you add "*gali gali.*" By that time I had already made my own small Jumli to Nepali dictionary.

I had to react after hearing such an emotional plea from Tara. Even though my current position didn't allow me to treat patients, as a nurse I felt obliged to help. I couldn't sit there saying it was not in my job description.

I followed her.

The emergency room was 50-60 metres away. I rushed there with Tara and checked the patient. She didn't have diarrhoea. She was bleeding and unconscious due to retained placenta after delivery. It turned out that in Jumli dialect even bleeding is referred as *pakhala*, which means diarrhoea in Nepali.

I had treated many patients like this when I worked in the Bharatpur Hospital as an anaesthetic nurse. Bleeding can be stopped in anywhere from 30 seconds to 20 minutes. This can be done at home as well. Generally, we recommend a medicine that contracts the uterus and stops the bleeding. We could also save the patient with a blood transfusion but there was no blood, syringe or IV fluid available. Blood transfusion and surgery were out of imagination.

I sent someone to see if any of the private clinics outside could help us but to no avail.

I couldn't see any alternative but to take the patient down

to an urban centre like Surkhet or Nepalganj. But the family didn't have any money. Flying two of them, the patient and a care-giver, would have cost at least Rs 6000. I didn't have enough money to help. The more time we delayed, the more critical the patient's condition would become. So I took what money I had and asked other friends to contribute until I had Rs 6000. Then we took the patient and her care-giver to the airport.

Unfortunately, the helicopter had already left.

The lady didn't survive.

I couldn't sleep that night. The image of the woman dying in front of me kept flashing before my eyes. I feel that she and her grieving relatives were standing nearby and I was terrified. I looked around the room but it was empty. I felt empty as well. Damn! I had come here to do something significant and hadn't been able to save that one patient. I saw my mother in that lady's face and wanted to cry.

These events had a profound effect on me. I thought how often those things happened in Jumla and how difficult it was to work in the area of health services in a place where one mother died every 30 minutes.

If our work was to have any impact we needed an operating theatre, a blood bank and emergency funds. Only after seeing that put in place would my stay in Jumla be meaningful. It would be better to leave Jumla altogether than to see patients dying needlessly every day, and dying a little with them.

But the thought of leaving Jumla made me feel cold. I felt as if my feet couldn't support my body. I lay down on my bed, closed my eyes and saw my father's face.

"Daughter, people poorer than us live in Jumla. When you become big, you have to serve them."

I had happily answered, "Yes, Father."

I opened my eyes.

It felt as if my father was helping me. My body started to warm up. Right then I decided I would not run away. I would fight to solve the problems and I would win.

My father always showed me the right way. Jumla needed me because people poorer than I lived there.

2

MY LOVELY JUMLA

At the highest point was the police station with the army barracks just below it. At a much lower point was the airport. Next to the runway, flowed the Tila River. At the junction of the airport, Karnali Technical Institute and Mahatgaun was a small bazaar.

This was Khalanga, the district headquarters of Jumla.

To the north of the bazaar were gently rising hills and behind them were enormous mountains called Danphe Lek. On the east was flat land beside the banks of the Tila River. We would go through the hills to visit popular places like Pandav Cave, Nagarkot and Haat Sinja. Haat Sinja is also known as Khas, the birthplace of the Nepali language. In the east, the sun made the top of Mt Kanjirowa glow like gold early in the morning and in the evening.

As the Human Resource Development Officer, my job was to train doctors and nurses in safe maternal health care practices. After evaluating the knowledge of local health workers, I was responsible for training them myself or sending them to other places for training. I was also responsible for capacity building in organisations and people who were involved in maternity services. For that, I had to communicate with the locals. I used to go to *panighatta* – the watermill –where I met both *dalit* and non-*dalit* women. I talked with them. I ate with them the tasty *rota*s and *chapattis* made from millet flour with salt and pepper that they brought for lunch. Sometimes I used to smoke *chillum* with them.

I wanted to really live in the Jumla my father had introduced me to. I wanted to explore the lifestyle of the Jumli people. I wanted to rise above just fulfilling the responsibilities of my job and do something really significant for them. Therefore, I was a Human Resource Development Officer only within the confines of our single-room office. At other times, I used to be a community mobiliser, nurse, doctor, teacher, domiciliary midwife and helper, among other things. I believe I did all these things to the best of my ability.

The advantage of this was that I got a closer view of Jumla – its society, culture, and the lifestyle of the Jumli people – and developed a much better understanding of it than the people who came here just to complete their service and then left complaining about the poverty and destitution.

Jumla and the Jumli people have taught me lessons that even a million books couldn't teach.

It's true that all places have their own unique society, culture and lifestyle. Jumla's are special. Lots of festivals, big and small, occur throughout the year, including *Sainik Jatra* (Soldier's Day), *Ropain Jatra* (celebration of the first planting) and many others. Just counting the number of festivals, Jumla looks similar to Kathmandu. However, the style of celebrating is completely different. In Kathmandu, even small festivals are celebrated like weddings. In Jumla, however, the only similarity to that is that people look like the crying family of the bride who has just seen their daughter off. I couldn't understand why Jumli people weren't jolly during their festivals, instead of looking like they were being compelled to pay a price for remoteness or a tax on poverty. Sometimes I felt the festivals were only meaningful to the handful of relatively wealthy people in Jumla.

Those who think they are advantaged or disadvantaged just because of caste should come and visit Jumla. It isn't just *dalits* or so-called lower caste people who suffer. Higher caste people and those who are supposedly favoured by the government such as *brahmins* and *chhetris* also have to work very hard in order to get even basic food and clothing. Without looking at a census, I can say from my experience that in Jumla the majority of people are *brahmins*, *chhetris* and *dalits*. There are also Mugalis who migrated from neighbouring district Mugu and who, in my experience, are just as poor.

My father said people in Jumla prayed in the Chandannath and Bhairavnath temples near the river. Once, while I was going to the temple, I went to the river to get some water but it was frozen. I broke the ice with a stone and then heated it to make water.

Jumli people still pray in Chandannath and Bhairavnath. During *Dashain*, both the temples get cleaned and the deities are washed. People believe in Chandannath as God and believe he grants wishes. The people in Jumla must have wished for lots of things for many generations. How many wishes have come true I don't know, but they haven't stopped wishing.

Even though I didn't see the entire river frozen as my father had, the cold weather made me long for home at first. Winter started even before *Dashain*, by mid-July. After *Tihar*, it snowed from mid-November until April. During my morning walks, I started seeing ice in different places.

For the first time in my life, I saw the national bird, Danphe, in Jumla. I saw the Danphe but I also saw people hunting and eating the bird although that's technically illegal in Nepal. When it started to snow, the birds came towards human settlements for shelter and people hunted them. The hunters were the same people who were supposed to arrest hunters! I heard that people held parties with Danphe meat. I didn't like that.

I love the language of Jumla. Interestingly, in the Jumli language, there are no special pronouns for use when referring to younger and older people, just like in English. In Nepali, we use *"tan"* for younger people, *"timi"* for friends, and *"tapain"* and *"hajur"* for seniors. In English it's easy: everybody is "you." There is no high or low language. Jumli is also like that. If we wanted to ask "What are you doing?" regardless of the age of the person, we could ask, *"Tumin ke gadda chhau?"*

Most of the women wore *cholo* – blouse – and sari. A shawl was on their heads. Women used to wear their shawls like the people in the Tarai wearing *"ghum"* during the rainy season. If there were some elderly people or people they looked up to, they would bring the shawl down to their eyes as a gesture of respect. Then they would put the shawl around their ears and catch it with their mouths. In Jumli language, this was called "*ghumcho*." For me, this tradition resembled the ladies in the Tarai wearing *ghunghat* or Muslim ladies wearing burkas.

Men generally wore *daura-suruwal* – traditional shirt and pants – with a jacket. Most of them wore traditional hats called topis. Only a few traditional clothes made from sheep's wool could be found in the bazaar. When I was in Kathmandu, I saw this same clothing on the Jumli people there. There were only a few houses, belonging to businessmen, community leaders and officers, which were reinforced concrete structures. Most of the other houses were made of mud and stone. Mud was also spread on the roof. Mud protects against snow and makes the houses warm. Most of the houses had two storeys. Cattle were kept on the ground floor and people lived on the first floor.

During sickness, the people's first inclination was to turn to shamans rather than the hospital. They didn't want to go to the hospital – no matter how sick they were and, if they did come to the hospital, it was always as a last resort. The weirdest thing I came across was the belief that a pregnant woman shouldn't cross a river because that would make the gods angry and bring bad luck to the community. Another belief prevented menstruating women from touching the base of the home. This meant, in practice, that they were not allowed to stay in the house. They, however, were sent to live in *chhaupadi* – a shelter outside the house – in seclusion for some days. There were a plethora of such practices.

There was a marked preference for boys over girls but after the birth people didn't care too much about that when it came to raising their kids. Unable to bear the thought of going through labour again, the women would say "I will not give birth again" but they continued to have babies every year. The kids grew up playing in the mud and roaming the mountains. Dreaming about the future is done by those who have a future. In Jumla, where it was a boon just to have enough food to eat, who thought beyond today?

There was a huge difference in lifestyle between men and women. However educated the men might be, they talked about equality between the sexes only outside their homes. Inside their home, their wives and daughters were still treated like slaves from history books and religious texts. Going from home to home, I felt the women were living the life of animals, not only in the houses of ignorant and uneducated people but also in the homes of educated families. The men walked around town while their women worked hard in their houses even with cracked feet. They never removed their *ghumcho* from their faces.

Leaders, officers, journalists and nurses who talked big outside still practiced and followed *chhaupadi*, a practice of periodic ostracisation whereby women were not supposed to eat rice, milk, or meat during menstruation. They were not allowed to meet their friends. They couldn't touch plants or vegetables and fruits or go near pregnant women or children. Not to mention temples. They kept a distance from the temples and didn't even look at them, as if it were a sin.

Oh my God! I was devastated to see these practices.

In this modern age, when we can light our houses in the night, Jumla was still living in pitch-blackness. Not darkness because of the absence of light but because of the absence of knowledge. It was the darkness of ignorance.

The people in Jumla liked chewing gum a lot, maybe trying to forget about the darkness in which they were living. I saw a lot of women popping bubble gum while carrying loads of stones. Were they trying to suppress anger by chewing?

Another common method to relieve their pain was alcohol consumption. There was huge demand of both homemade moonshine and imported alcohol from Nepalganj and Surkhet. I have seen officers coming to work drunk. I have met police on duty when not sober. Rice productivity is very low. People die from hunger. But alcohol is made from the rice that the government distributes as aid. What should we call this, ignorance or a result of foreign dependency?

"Should you be doing this?" I asked many.

They replied without hesitation, "Without alcohol, our body doesn't warm up."

It's all right to warm up the body but alcohol also fires up the mind leading to fights and violence, and the victims are usually women.

Where alcohol consumption was so common, tobacco was as well, though not necessarily cigarettes. They also smoke *sulpha* – a mixture of tobacco and cannabis products, to which many women were addicted. It was also quite normal to smoke *chillum* made from local tobacco. Friends from the Mrigendra Health Organisation have told me that Jumla is among the districts where health is mostly severely affected by smoking.

However, we can't single out tobacco as the only cause of smoke-related health problems. Electricity hadn't reached many places in the district. Wood, mostly pinewood, was used to cook and to give warmth. Firewood leads to black smoke which is very harmful. There were some foreign organisations that promoted smokeless stoves but their reach was only into hotels and the homes of the rich.

The other problem in Jumla was the absence of government officials. They got involved in travel and training or were temporarily transferred to urban centres like Nepalganj, Surkhet or Kathmandu. Offices were run by the junior officers acting in the position and sometimes they weren't present either and the responsibilities fell on the next in charge. I met government officers who didn't come back even after five months of holidays. However, did the people get better service in offices where the officers stayed for all 12 months of the year? I doubt it. Corruption was a plague in Jumla and influential people got preferential access to health services, airplane seats and even in government bidding. Even I behaved in a similar way when I got my seat on the helicopter while there were so many other people waiting for tickets.

Never before in my life had I encountered such a detrimental custom.

But every cloud has a silver lining and Jumla was no exception. Even though Jumla had the pain of poverty, ignorance, hunger, disease, superstition and feudalism, it was, and is, blessed with the bounty of nature. Jumla is home to prized *yarsagumba* (*Cordyceps sinensis*), morel, medicinal plants, *paanch aunle* (*Dactylorhiza hatagirea*) and red rice. There are also a lot of other herbs that we haven't been able to identify yet.

Yarsagumba was the gold of Jumla. Lending and giving was based on it. There was a common saying that, when taking out a loan, it would be repaid during the season of yarsagumba. Buying it was not difficult at all. I paid Rs 47 to buy one *yarsagumba*. Morel – locally called *gucchi chyau* – cost Rs 10-15 apiece whereas the same mushroom when it reached Nepalganj would cost Rs 10,000 per kg, Rs 15,000 in New Delhi and Rs 20,000 in Japan, so the locals said. I liked the taste of morel very much. It can be eaten like a vegetable and also mixed in noodles. Father talked a lot about the red rice of Jumla. From the day I started eating this rice, which grows at the highest altitude on earth, I felt as if my height had increased by an inch.

I remember when we were kids, lots of *bhotinis* – women from the high mountains – used to sell us sugary food that cost Rs 1 or 2. We ate them as *shilajit*. I was surprised to see that in Jumla as well. It had a strong aroma and even a single drop could make a glass of milk turn black.

There is so much to Jumla. But why don't we talk about the good things? Why are only the bad things about Jumla ever mentioned? Why do we just take national pride in Mount Everest and Lumbini? Isn't *yarsagumba* something to be proud of as well? Aren't the medicinal herbs in Jumla at least as important as the oil of the Arabs?

"Coming to Jumla just to earn money," we teased newcomers. Their intention was to earn money without doing any work. I didn't have an answer to that when I first arrived but today I would say "What can I take from Jumla?" Why is Jumla so down-trodden when it could bring in a lot of money for the whole country? When Jumla's resources are properly exploited, then its economy will improve and life in the district will get better.

This is my firm belief, not just my hope, because the longer I stayed and the closer I came to the community, I realised

Jumla was not poor. In fact, it was potentially extremely rich.

This was the difference in the pictures of Jumla that my father and I saw. We were poor because we had nothing. Jumla had everything but was still poor. It reminded me of the proverbial saying – the musk deer doesn't realise that it carries the redolent musk gland but runs in the forest to find the aroma.

The day Jumla realises its potential, I will tell my daughter, "People richer than us live in Jumla."

Jumla gave me a new direction in my life. Jumla showed me new dreams.

More than that, it gave me the love that made me forget about my home and made Jumla my home away from home.

It's said there is one difference between home and a hotel: in a hotel even after having *chauraasi vyanjan* – 84 varieties – in a meal, we still feel hungry. At home, however deprived we may be, we feel content.

I had heard this saying since my childhood but after I came to Jumla I found it wasn't true.

I stayed in the Everest Hotel in Bijayanagar. Since it had the same name as the five-star hotel in Kathmandu, we used to call it "Jumla's Five-Star Hotel" though only the name was the same.

It had a wooden ladder which made a lot of noise when somebody went up or down. The rooms were small and the restroom was outside. I have exerted great self-control

43

many times just to avoid going out into the cold night. The restroom was also not modern. It was basically just a big hole in the ground with a cement floor and walls.

However, the food in the hotel was very good and it was clean. But facilities, food and cleanliness aren't the only things that make a hotel good. Hospitality has a part to play and the owners of the hotel, Sunil *dai* and Goma *bhauju*, became like family to me. They were like my own brother and sister-in-law, or maybe even closer. They had four children. The kids called me *"Fupu"* (Father's sister). After I went there, Goma *bhauju*'s sister-in-law had a daughter. She was very close to me. Whenever she heard my voice in the evening, she would come to sit on my lap. Her grandmother took very good care of me, maybe because I was a single lady who was working there alone.

"Why did you leave your home and come here during war, *nani?*" the grandmother asked me, "Aren't you afraid?"

"You are here for me, so why should I be afraid?" I replied.

Living among the owner's family made me forget that I was living in a hotel. I felt I was at home.

I used to bring my colleagues to the hotel for lunch or coffee and tea. Colleagues from Surkhet, Bardiya and Kathmandu also came to stay at the hotel sometimes. The owners treated my guests as family. But the person had to be good. This was not because the owners were mean-spirited but because the Maoist insurgency and the government's response were getting stronger every day and we couldn't trust anyone on face value anymore. We would only trust people when we knew more about them. Otherwise, we had constant fear generated by both the army and the Maoists.

Janaki from the Women's Development Office used to come to stay with me. Later, she was transferred. A nurse from Mahatgaun also came occasionally. Her husband was into politics and stayed away from home most of the time. They didn't have any kids. Poor her, she didn't have anyone to talk to at home. We had many things in common and she was happy to be around me. At least she didn't have to stay alone in her room during a time of conflict.

That applied equally to me.

In winter, I needed hot water to take a shower and to wash my clothes. Stored water would freeze during the night. We were able to use it only after melting it with hot water. Goma *bhauju* used to bring me warm water daily. I also helped her to do kitchen chores. I would make tea in the morning and put it in a thermos flask for them. I also cut vegetables. I kept myself busy during the morning and evenings by helping them.

We started talking about our personal lives as well. She shared her experiences and feelings about her father's oppressive behaviour towards her, mistreatment by her maternal uncle and aunt, and poverty with me. I realised there was a lot of sorrow hidden behind her smile.

Carrying so many burdens in life, people in Jumla looked much older than their actual age. Even now the average life expectancy of people in the Karnali region is only 37 years and many live for even less. The more sorrow in life, the more wrinkles on one's face and Goma *bhauju*'s face was no different.

I taught her various skills to make her more independent. She had an interest in learning. If I was in my room, she would come in and start reading "*Ka, Kha...*" Her face glowed whenever she learned a new letter of the alphabet. Her smile instantaneously made me happy. I thought, many stars like her might have gone dark before even having a chance to shine in Jumla.

Then again, I thought, the Maoist insurgency didn't let any stars grow and shine at all.

I was happy with my stay at the Everest Hotel. I was satisfied. I didn't have any fears.

However, one day a call came from the administration department in Kathmandu: "Do not stay in that hotel. Either stay in the hospital's quarters or find somewhere else."

"Why?" I asked.

"That hotel is near the police station. It could be risky," they said. "The Maoists are attacking police stations and army barracks. If they attack there, then the Everest Hotel will also be affected. They might even take the hotel as a vantage point during an attack."

For the first time, I was petrified.

3

LIFE IN FEAR

"You have a technical background. You will be very useful to them. You are the only one in the district from whom they can gain an advantage."

Goma *bhauju* tried to warn me. But this created havoc inside me. I started to think lots of things when I was alone in my room. The smallest sound outside would wake me up.

I arrived in Jumla in 2001 when the Maoist conflict was still on-going. In Kathmandu, I had read news about shootings and bombings carried out by the Maoists. My friends had advised me not to go to Jumla because of them. But knowing all that, I still came to Jumla. Now, however, fear took on a new meaning. I tried to harden myself but there was a huge difference between listening to news of conflict happening far away and actually experiencing it. Hearing the news made me anxious for a little while but the fear of being actually in the news made me apprehensive day and night.

After coming to Jumla, I had started to see the effect of the conflict. I felt Jumla was much more insecure than

I had imagined it would be by reading the newspapers in Kathmandu.

At first, nobody opened up to me about it. They didn't say anything. They used to think that a girl from an urban center like Chitwan wouldn't last in such a remote place. One day, they thought, she'll leave her job and go away. I proved everyone who thought that wrong. People came to believe in my work ethic and commitment.

And they started to share their fears with me as well.

I would see the same people in different states of mind on the same day. Usually, businesspeople and officers visited the temple of Chandannath at the start of the day. They were very energetic in the morning and their faces looked bright. As the day progressed, however, they started to become lethargic and, as darkness set in, despondency could be seen in their faces. Government officers always rushed to get home from work early. The market used to close at dusk. There would be more dogs and less people on the streets. A curfew in the town was a common thing. Even when a curfew wasn't in place, the town would feel like it was under curfew.

We used to hear about attacks by the Maoists on a daily basis. People in touch with the DAO, police and the army brought news of new attacks every day. Due to their fear of the Maoists, the political leaders and big merchants had already moved away. Sometimes they came back without informing anyone, finished their tasks in a day or two and then disappeared discreetly again.

Some rising local leaders didn't always stay in the same house. They rotated their stays in the homes of their relatives, neighbours and friends. They feared that if they stayed in the same place for too long the Maoists would find out. While returning from the office, I saw many leaders hurrying to get to somebody's home, carrying their dinners with them.

I wore day clothes when I went to bed at night because, if the Maoists came to kidnap me, I wouldn't have time to change out of my nightdress before they came through the door. The door was weak, made from pine. I felt as if I could break the door down with my own fists. No need to talk about the strength of Maoist fighters. Goma *bhauju* and her husband had also suggested that the scenario of finding a woman alone in her nightdress might lead to other incidents, so it was better to sleep fully clothed.

I did all this just to calm my mind. The day the Maoists attacked, who knew if I would even survive?

For security reasons, buying shoes made of fabric was banned in the town because they could be used by the Maoists. Even if somebody bought the shoes for themselves, they would be looked on with suspicion in case they had bought the shoes for the Maoists. We had to list the number of people in the family in order to buy ready-to-eat foods like biscuits and noodles. If we bought more than was needed for the family we had to explain ourselves at the DAO. We had to get permission from the DAO if we needed to buy foodstuff for parties.

We had started to build an operating theatre. In order to buy the things that were needed we had to get a letter of support from the hospital and permission from both the DAO and the army. Since our programme was about maternal and child health care, it was not too difficult to get permission. However, it would have been extremely difficult for the general public to get such permission.

Every person along with their belongings who came from Surkhet and Nepalganj had to go through checks along the way by the police and the armed forces. What was the purchasing power of Jumlis? What could they bring back with them? I have seen security personnel throwing Jumlis' goods away. The hotel where I stayed was just 50 meters from the district police station. I saw everything from the windows – the police on security alert and the oppressive treatment of innocent citizens in the name of security.

Also for security reasons we were unable to send medicines to health sub-posts in the districts. The fear that the Maoists might use them prompted a ban on bringing in essential medicines. The administration took on that role and would bring medicines in by its own means but only after repeated requests from the health center. Health personnel in the health sub-posts always complained, "We don't even have supplies of basic medicines. What's the point of us being here?"

Their complaint was fair enough. How could they treat patients when they didn't even have a single paracetamol tablet? Health personnel aren't magicians who treat patients by waving wands and doing tricks. However, it must be said that pressure from the Maoists was also one of the factors that made them ask for more supplies. They had to work among the rebels who would threaten them, demanding medicines. As a result, they had to make up different stories in order to be sent more supplies. If nothing else worked, they would whisper, "The Maoists are demanding these medicines. We can't go back without them."

We understood. There was no other way. Either that or we had to close down the health center or knowingly let our colleagues be killed.

I used to get emotional when I was caught in a dilemma between my responsibility as an administrator and my obligation towards my colleagues. I even got furious sometimes.

Such problems also arose in the Safe Motherhood training programme. Since it was the first year of the programme, we had to bring the health workers in from the villages and train them appropriately. But how could we ask them to come during such times of terror and insecurity? When I heard their stories of how they had managed to come to the district capital, it made me feel really bad. At that time, travelling between the capital and the villages was much more difficult than travelling on the highways. It was like walking on the edge of a sword.

We had to be afraid of the security personnel, as well as the Maoists. In the capital, security personnel kept a log of our names and, in the villages, the Maoists kept the log. Both sides could interrogate innocent people on suspicion of spying. They could even beat us, arrest us, kidnap us and take our lives. This was why the trainees told me many times, "Sister, please don't ask us to come for training. It's more difficult to come to the capital than it is to go abroad." To come to the capital, they had to get permission from the Maoists, just like getting a visa. If by any chance the letter of permission was found by the security personnel, then they would be stuck in a nightmare. The security personnel would immediately arrest them and charge them with espionage. My friends said that before entering the capital, they made markings on stones or trees and hid the permission letter there. When they returned, they collected the letter on the way. If by any chance they forgot the letter or if it was lost or ruined by the weather, then they would be beaten by the Maoists when they returned to their home villages. Their lives were on the line.

After hearing such horror stories, how could we ask anyone to risk their lives just for training?

If one of their comrades was critically ill, the Maoists would come to the hospital themselves sometimes, posing as civilians. We didn't acknowledge that we knew who they were and would treat the patients. Before departing, they would shake our hands very tightly and with force as if to show us who they were. After that we would be anxious about getting into trouble with the army. Some of my colleagues had been taken into custody for just such reasons. Some others had to be evacuated. Many times I felt trapped between the army and the Maoists.

Once, during a training session, I was taking a stroll in a village and came to a place where the Maoists were organising a programme. They immediately surrounded me.

"I'm a nurse. I'm here giving training," I repeatedly said, "I don't have anything."

They didn't listen to me. Searching all my belongings, they found nothing more than medicines. "Give us money," they said but I didn't have any cash.

Then they pressured me to speak as part of their programme. I said, "I don't know what to say. I just know how to talk about safe pregnancy and child birth. Should I speak about that?"

They scolded me. Then they kept me captive for four hours before releasing me.

When we visited the villages, we were in constant fear of the Maoists and, after returning from the villages, the army used to interrogate us.

Once, when it was dusk already, I was on the verandah of the hospital when a group of soldiers came and surrounded it.

"You are being called by our Major to come to the barracks," one soldier told me.

"Why?" I asked.

"The Major is sick."

I was in a dilemma. I was worried. But still I didn't lose my courage.

"If he's sick, then bring him here," I said. "There's no equipment in the barracks. We can take better care of him here. And if there's anything else, then bring a warrant. I am not moving from here without a warrant."

Since I walked from village to village, they had assumed I must have important information about the Maoists. They questioned me for an hour before leaving.

That was the way we lived our lives.

As the war intensified, we saw more police and soldiers making their rounds than we saw children playing in the bazaar. We stopped hearing the sound of the school bell. Instead we started to get used to the sound of explosions and gunshots. The *diyos* – oil lamps – in the temple of Chandannath grew dimmer. We saw fire strikes on Bohoragaun across the Tila River every day.

Fear was so prevalent that we were terrified by any loud noise, thinking it was a bomb blast. We pricked up our ears even at the sound of a creaking door. We had to get permission from the DAO to play music at a wedding or in any other programme. The Administration also ordered us to complete any programmes before curfew. There was a tradition of lighting *diyos* in the evening like *Tihar* on the first day of Shrawan. The Administration banned it so we had to light *diyo*s in the afternoon.

We were also not allowed to walk or meet in groups. If the army or police saw people in groups, they would interrogate them for quite a long time. Due to security constraints, it had started to become difficult to bring patients to the hospital. If the patient was critical, we had to inform the police and then bring the patient to the hospital under their supervision. There were many cases of infants dying before birth because of this regime.

Every day there were more and more rumours: the Maoists were preparing to attack Khalanga Bazaar; they were taking one person from each home; baskets were being made day and night to carry injured fighters. Sometimes there were rumours that they had already built bunkers. Sometimes we heard that the Maoists had come up to Tatopani, closer to the district headquarters.

It felt as if all the people in Khalanga Bazaar were walking on hot coals. We were counting every breath and heartbeat. It would have been easier to die quickly. Dying second by second was much more painful. Meeting up with people we knew made us happy like a flower blooming in spring. Oh, he's alive! Thank God! If we didn't see someone for a few days, our hearts shrank like the withered flowers of winter. Maybe he had been killed in crossfire?

Saying "Good night" before sleeping took on a special significance which I have not experienced before or since because who knew whether we would see each other the next morning or not?

And every morning, after waking up alive, we looked at each other and hugged.

Then we smiled, "Congratulations! We survived another night."

21 May 2001

The Maoists attacked Dang. They started the raid by attacking the army barracks in the capital, Ghorahi. One Major, 15 regular soldiers and seven policemen were killed. Around 40 were injured. Seven Maoists also died. The Maoists succeeded in looting lots of weapons and ammunition from the barracks.

After this attack, the government declared a state of emergency. I was evacuated to Kathmandu.

At that time, I was in the process of taking exams for my Master of Arts in Sociology. I hadn't been able to prepare well for all the subjects. I had planned to take some time off from work specifically to prepare for the examinations but I hadn't been able to. I decided to take one exam while I was in Kathmandu and leave the rest for the next year.

I took the first exam in the Kirtipur Centre.

During that time, I heard news that there was a clash in Jumla. The Maoists had detonated a bomb in Sinhachaur. In response, the army started firing shots at 4 pm and continued throughout the night. Two civilians lost their lives. My office postponed my return date for security reasons. This was an advantage for me. I took all my exams for that year after all and passed.

When I returned to Jumla I found people were more cold and oppressed than ever before. There was the fear of death in everyone's eyes. No one trusted anyone. New faces were regarded with suspicion. Everybody weighed what they said in order to avoid trouble with either the Maoists or the army. I felt as if the people who were very close to me in the past also started keeping their distance.

During my childhood, I didn't fall asleep without listening to my father's stories about Jumla. After going there, I didn't fall asleep without hearing the sound of explosions or gunshots. After the state of emergency was declared, hearing explosions and gunshots in Jumla became as common as hearing the sound of car horns in big cities. People in other remote areas must have felt the same way.

The army used to fire rocket-launchers or machine guns in gaps of half an hour, one hour or sometimes every two-three hours in the evenings. Their intention was to scare off the Maoists if they were nearby. With this happening every day, even civilians had stopped being afraid of it so how would that have scared the Maoists?

However, if for some reason the firing was late or there was no firing, we would feel incomplete somehow. It felt like the silence in a home when the kids have gone to stay at their uncle's. We got so used to the explosions and gunshots that if we didn't hear them for a night we asked each other "What happened in the barracks?" Had the Maoists raided the barracks before the army started to fire?

Whenever we heard gunshots and bomb blasts from the barrack, we felt the soldiers were safe and, while the soldiers were safe, we felt we were also safe.

My background in nursing had taught me that music helps sleep to come. After coming to Jumla, I wasn't able to sleep without hearing the sounds of gunshots. I dubbed it the "music for sleeping." My colleagues laughed when they heard that. They also had similar feelings.

We were so used to it that we could differentiate between shots fired by the Maoists and shots fired by the security forces just by the sound. We could even differentiate between the shots fired by the police and the army. Next day we shared our guesses and realised how sharp our ears had become.

If the sound was *pat-pat* then we could tell that it was firing from police 303 rifles. Police officers didn't have any other firearms. If the *rat-a-tat* sound came continuously five or 10 times then it was a machine gun. If we could feel tremors along with the sound then we knew it was a rocket-launcher. That sound always made us very afraid as we waited for the next sound to come. Sometimes, if we were outside, we ran indoors and listened attentively.

There was only one reason to be outside at night - to use

the toilet. Indoor restrooms were rare. People were afraid to go out during the night, especially children and the elderly, so they made chamber pots from cut-off gallon bottles.

When the curfew began to be tightened, even going out to the toilet at the night was forbidden. The army started to use bright lights, dazzling the whole town. These lights were used to detect Maoist activities whenever there was firing in the hills, or when they heard chants like "Maoist Jindabad", or if some informant let the army know the Maoists had planned some kind of programme.

Sometimes there was firing along with the light. The army had difficulty in differentiating between Maoists and civilians at night so we were ordered not to go out after dark and to "manage toilets inside." How could we manage indoor toilets? We controlled ourselves during the night and stopped going out in the dark.

The army patrolled in the brightness of the light. As soon as we heard the sound of their boots, we were frightened and would congregate together. If we were outside, we ran indoors and quickly closed all the doors and windows. Then we lit a small *tuki* and stayed put. Sometimes we didn't even light the *tuki* and stayed in the dark.

Darkness had become part of our lives.

As the security situation deteriorated, organisations like ours and diplomatic missions started to implement security plans. A three-day security training programme was organised in Nepalganj. One expert from England came to Jumla to give us training. New Security Directors were employed. A phone tree containing the residential phone numbers of all officers was made. Security coordinators in the field were given satellite phones and the number was given to all of us.

If somebody's life was in danger, then a mechanism was in place to rent a helicopter to move them elsewhere. Life and accident insurance was introduced guaranteeing Rs 1.6 million if a person was killed or lost their limbs.

I felt sad to see these mechanisms introduced though they also made me laugh. I thought, aren't we just scratching the surface of the conflict? Should development workers like us have a "security" barrier between ourselves and the locals or should we coordinate with both the Maoists and the locals to implement our programmes? If a life was lost then what meaning would Rs 1.6 million have? These thoughts spun around in my head.

My mind was unstable. Jumla was unstable. My country was unstable.

While we development workers were shrinking back inside our secure perimeters, the Maoists launched yet another attack.

16 February 2002

Success in the attack on Dang prompted the Maoists to attack the police station and army barracks in Mangalsen, Achham. Fifty-two soldiers and 95 police died in the attack.

A letter came addressed to me from my office headquarters in Kathmandu. It said "Please leave the Everest Hotel as soon as possible and move to an alternative location. Otherwise, if anything happens the office will not be responsible and won't be obligated to provide any insurance pay-out."

I was furious.

Did I go there with the office guaranteeing my life? Whether in conflict or not, can anyone guarantee somebody's life? How could they say "If anything happens the office won't be responsible"? I didn't just come to the Everest Hotel off my own back. My office had suggested that this hotel was the safest place to stay in Jumla.

I felt, since we had been working continuously in Jumla even during the conflict, people from our organisation in Kathmandu were able to hold their heads up high at the national and international level. What perks and benefits they gained because of that I don't know. But they knew the situation in which we were working, caught between the security forces and the Maoists.

Most of the higher ranking officers in my office in Kathmandu had come to Jumla at least once. Even if they hadn't come, I don't believe they closed their eyes and ears when attacks in Jumla were reported in the news every day. Then, after knowing all this, how could they decide on such a matter without even consulting me? I had left my home to work for the country and to continue the programme. Was there no value to my sacrifice? I became disheartened whenever I thought about it.

When a human feels afraid, he needs his home. The love of the family acts as his shield. In order to keep my sanity and my confidence, I needed a stronger shield. The love and care I received from Sunil *dai*, Goma *bhauju*, Grandmother and the kids had protected and supported me throughout my time in Jumla.

On the days when Sunil *dai* started drinking at dusk, I would wait for him to admonish me about the Maoists. He was worried about my safety and always said, "Don't think that you can change Jumli people. Stay in the bazaar and work there. Don't get in the way of the Maoists."

I didn't follow his advice.

The Kathmandu office had also advised me not to leave Khalanga Bazaar. I was amazed. I had come here to work in the villages. What would I do just sitting in the bazaar? I believed it was better to return to Kathmandu than to hold up, shrinking from fear, in the bazaar.

"The problem is in the villages. What is there to do in the bazaar?" I told both Sunil *dai* and the Kathmandu office, "I am going to the villages. Let's see what the Maoists will do."

"What will they do? They will cut your throat," Sunil *dai* tried to intimidate me.

"Then let them cut my throat. I'm not afraid," I said.

Goma *bhauju* supported Sunil. She said the same thing to me every night with tears in her eyes. Just to avoid more drama, I would say, "I won't go, *Bhauju*."

Next morning, I would go towards the villages without letting them know.

After the state of emergency was declared, I started to get threats in the name of the Maoists. I even got threats relating to remuneration for attending training.

There had been a culture of not attending training but coming in at the end just to sign the attendance records and claim remuneration. Some, mostly those who were considered the elite, signed the attendance forms and received remuneration without even leaving home. I would not allow this to continue. I introduced a rule whereby remuneration would only be given to those who attended the training programmes from start to finish.

Since I was trying to break this pattern of unfairness and corruption, which had been in place for a long time, I was unpopular in the eyes of many people. They threatened me on the phone, "We are Maoists." Sometimes they warned me, "Give us the remuneration immediately, otherwise we will inform the Maoists."

They used to talk about this stuff with Sunil *dai*. They said to him, "Counsel the lady living at your place to do the right thing, otherwise it will be bad."

Many people tried extortion in the name of the Maoists. They asked for money or medicines but I gave nothing if it was inappropriate. I believed that as long as I followed the rules, I didn't have to worry, a belief I had learned from my father. Sunil *dai* was afraid however and fair enough. Which brother wouldn't be worried if somebody threatened his sister? And which brother wouldn't counsel his sister for her own safety?

Sunil *dai* was like that, though he couldn't speak out to me without getting drunk first. I, on the other hand, wouldn't take his talk seriously when he was drunk and, in fact, tried not to be around him when he was drinking. After returning from the hospital, I would just go to my room saying I had a headache.

One day after finishing a discussion programme, I came into my office. There was a note on the table with my name on it. It said: "Don't try to be too clever. Leave Jumla within 24 hours, otherwise we will kill you." It was signed "Maoists."

I didn't talk to anyone about this note. After two or three days, there was a call for me in the reception of the hotel. I picked up the phone and somebody started to threaten me in similar language. Sunil *dai* listened to this conversation on the extension.

After this, Sunil *dai*, Goma *bhauju*, and Grandmother became even more worried. Under pressure from them, I started to live in their accommodation instead of my room in the hotel. Grandmother waited for me until I came home in the evening. After seeing me coming, she would silently go upstairs. If I was late, Sunil *dai* sent his kids to look for me. Sometimes the kids came up to the hospital to get me or Sunil *dai* himself would stroll around the streets just to make sure I arrived home safely. He didn't say anything and as soon as he saw me coming towards home, he would return.

Letters continued to arrive from the Kathmandu office but I was not going to leave the love and support of the Everest family who took care of me just like my own family. I stayed silent without replying. I didn't even notify the hospital. There was no way I would tell this to my family at home. If they knew there was such a high risk, they wouldn't have allowed me live in the whole of Karnali zone, let alone the Everest Hotel, Khalanga Bazaar or Jumla district.

One day during a vacation at my own family home, I visited my eldest sister. She was upset about me leaving home to go to Jumla.

"There's no phone, it's very far, there's no road access, every day we hear news about attacks, kidnapping, and murder by Maoists. Why would you go to a place like that?" she asked.

I reminded her of our father's words.

"Did Father tell you to go there to get killed?" she said angrily. "Go when it's more peaceful. I won't stop you then."

"It's my job, sis," I said. "If I mind my own business, nothing will happen to me."

"You don't have to do work like that" she said, her anger increasing. "Don't you have enough to eat that you have to do work like that? If that's the case, I'll send you enough money to eat by raising my chickens."

My sister had started to raise poultry at that time. She was very concerned about my future. There was no way I could win her over logically so I joked, "Don't you need more chickens? If something happens to me then I get Rs 1.6 million in insurance money. You can buy a lot of chickens with that."

I hadn't even completed my sentence before she threw a maize cob at me. I dodged.

Tears were rolling down her cheeks. I went closer and hugged her.

"Why are you worried, Sister? Nothing will happen to me," I started to console her but she just continued crying without saying anything. My eyes were also full of tears.

I had gone to Jumla, disregarding the tears shed by my loved ones, on the way paved by my father and I was not going to give up. But to get through my stay in Jumla, the love of my adopted family at the Everest Hotel was crucial. Moreover, whatever security reasons the Kathmandu office had cited for me moving out of the hotel were the very same reasons why I should stay. I was strong because I had the support of my adopted local family.

No one could attack without a reason or raise their voice against me. There was no guarantee that I would be safer in another place even if I decided to move out.

Even after explaining all these things, the unrelenting position of the Kathmandu office angered me but I remained undaunted.

I did not leave the Everest Hotel.

After a long space of time, when I was in Kathmandu, a member of the administration staff asked me, "Where is your room now?"

"Don't worry! My family won't have to claim the insurance money," I replied smiling.

4

REINCARNATION

A large group of human rights activists came to Jumla in the first week of August 2002. Sudeep Pathak, head of the Nepal Human Rights Organisation, was also in the group.

They also stayed in the Everest Hotel. I didn't have much interaction with the guests. They stayed in the room I used to stay in before I moved into Sunil *dai*'s private accommodation. But I knew Sudeep so one evening I asked him about the security situation in Jumla.

During that time, there was a strong rumour that the Maoists were targeting Jumla after their attacks on Dang and Achham.

"The Maoists have already attacked Sindhuli, Okhaldhunga, Arghakhanchi, Dang, Achham and Syangja among their 10 targeted districts," he said. "Now there's scuttlebutt that they are planning to attack Jumla. An initiative for talks has started. If possible, it might be better for you to fly to Kathmandu or go outside Jumla."

I became cold.

I thought – I'm not from Jumla so I might be able to go down from here but what about Sunil *dai*, Goma *bhauju*, Grandmother and the kids? Where would they go?

But then, where was it safe? The Maoist conflict had made the whole nation insecure. Should I leave the nation?

I decided again that I wouldn't go anywhere but wait and see what happened.

The Maoists had announced a Nepal *banda* – a country-wide general strike – 10,11 and 12 November.

There were rumours all over Khalanga Bazaar. Some said there wouldn't be any attacks during a Nepal *banda*. Others claimed this was the Maoists' preparatory time and then they would attack.

I had come to Jumla from Surkhet after two days of *Bhaitika*. It had already started to snow in October that year. This was the first time in 20 years it had snowed so early. A slim hope that the Maoists wouldn't attack when it was snowing was building inside me. "It will be difficult to walk in the snow," said the locals, "How could the Maoists attack?"

I thought the same thing.

On 14 November, I had to take part in a programme called "Foundation for Change". The Chief District Officer (CDO), Local Development Officer (LDO), District Superintendent of Police (DSP) and other influential people were also present. I was the moderator.

The programme was organised right across from the Everest Hotel. We were working in groups. I, CDO Damodar Pant, DSP Bijeshwor Ghimire and LDO Hari Bashistha and few others were on the rooftop making plans.

Pant proposed to make a waiting room in the hospital. He said, "If only life wasn't so insecure, we could do a lot more. But what can we do when the security situation gives us problems all the time?"

As he spoke, he became very serious.

I looked at his face and knew he was deeply troubled.

The programme was completed and everyone had gone home. I was planning to go down to Surkhet early the next morning. It was almost time for the curfew to start. When I went out from Jumla, I used to take letters, money or other things from there, not just for my own family but on behalf of other people as well, including my colleagues at the hospital.

The programme in Surkhet was already set up so I had to go. Friends at the hospital didn't like the idea. When I planned to go to Surkhet, Sunil *dai*, Goma *bhauju* and the kids became sad as well.

As I left the hospital, everyone wished me a safe trip but it sounded as though their hearts were heavy.

I was not very happy either though I didn't know why. I was just baffled. I said, "Thank you. I'll be back as soon as I finish the work."

I came home and had dinner with Sunil *dai*'s family.

We were eating at about 9 pm when we heard a bang. It was very loud but we felt it wasn't close.

"Today they've bombed somewhere far away," I said.

We didn't want to talk about it so we ate our dinner and, as usual, started watching TV. During that time, Nepal Television had started to broadcast in Khalanga Bazaar. The

TV tower was located next to the police station. The picture was not very clear, however, and that night it was even worse than usual. It was difficult to recognise faces on the screen.

The news was on and we watched or, to be more accurate, we listened with our eyes elsewhere. Goma *bhauju* and I both dozed off on the floor. We woke up after some time. A patriotic song was playing.

> *"Where there are Buddha's eyes*
> *Clean, serene, and beautiful*
> *There is a peaceful place*
> *My beautiful nation"*

The accompanying video had a clip from Sinhachaur, Jumla. Goma *bhauju* shouted, gesturing at the TV. I recognised the familiar place.

We were all smiling.

It was 10 pm already. I didn't want to go to my room. But I had to go. I couldn't just stay there all night. Moreover, I had to leave for Surkhet early the next morning.

I stood up to go to my room. I wanted to pee so I went outside even despite the curfew. There was an open verandah in between my room and Sunil *dai*'s room. They saw me going out and Sunil *dai* started to yell at me. I kept silent and went downstairs. I had gone outside to pee during curfew on other nights but on that night I don't know why but I felt afraid. I peed and scurried back to my room. I sat on the bed, listening carefully for any sounds. But the only sound I could hear was dogs barking. I didn't hear any bombs or gunshots.

I felt relieved.

I picked up a book, lay on my bed and started reading.

I had only read a few pages when I heard someone outside moving near the toilet. I heard someone coughing.

After that I couldn't concentrate on the book. I leaned my head towards Sunil *dai*'s room but I didn't hear anything. Everything was silent. My heartbeat grew louder. I stood up and left the book on the pillow. I squatted on the bed. Who could be outside? Who was walking outside during curfew? I had just come from there and I didn't see anyone. Were they police on patrol or had the Maoists finally come?

I had such questions in my mind, when I heard machinegun fire. It came from so close that I thought the shots were fired right above my head.

I quickly turned off the light.

It was cold at that time so I used two quilts and two blankets. I used the blankets instead of sheets and covered myself with the quilts. I hugged my quilt and lay down. I wondered, was this sound of shooting similar to other days or was there a real crossfire?

I hadn't even finished thinking about that when loud firing began. The army barracks returned fire. *Rat-a-tat-tat*. The sound of gunshots came from all directions.

I had no doubt the Maoists had attacked.

In such a situation it was risky to stay on top of the bed. I had learned in security training that I should position myself behind strong walls. But I didn't want to get up from my bed. I felt sure I was not going to survive in any case so, instead of being afraid, I started to listen to the sound of the crossfire. But I had covered my face completely with my quilt as if it could block both gunshots and bombs. Launchers were used by both the Maoists and the security personnel. A ball of fire came over the roof from one direction and then the other. There was continuous gunfire and I heard someone shouting "Arun! Arun!"

Then things calmed down for a while. The rocket attacks stopped. There were just a few popping sounds. I felt they were shots fired by the police. Again, I heard someone shouting "Arun! Arun!". Then the firing started again and the fireballs began flying from one direction or another across the roof.

Who was Arun? Was he the Maoist commander? There was no way I could look out the window. From the sound of the gunfire, I could guess there was heavy fighting in the field outside.

My room faced towards the road, opposite the door of the police station. There were two large windows in that wall. Shots being fired into the wall and roof sounded just like popping popcorn. I was sure they would penetrate the walls.

As afraid as I had been when I heard rumours of the attack, I was not that frightened during the attack. What would I achieve by being frightened? All I could do was to stay securely where I was. My mind was completely blank. No idea came into my head except "Whatever happens, let it happen."

Bhanu Devkota lived in the room next to mine with his wife and son but he was alone that night. He and I didn't usually converse. We just smiled when we met each other in the street. But that night, with the shots falling like hailstones, he was terrified and crying. With a voice full of fear, he called out to me "Radha *didi*, Radha *didi*".

I heard him but I didn't reply. I realised he was expecting some sort of help from me. Sunil *dai* was also shouting "Radha, Radha" from across the verandah. I didn't reply to him either but just kept quiet and lay on my bed.

Just then Sunil *dai* came and knocked on my door.

I opened the door and he pulled me out of my room. Bhanu also came out.

The moon was shining brightly. From the verandah, I could see a mass of people from the DAO up to our house. The Maoist soldiers were like a swarm of locusts. One wave surged forward to be followed by another and another. The sound of gunfire and bombs exploding were coming from all sides and my eyes were dazzled by the flash that came when a gun was fired.

Sunil *dai* took me into his room. Goma *bhauju* was inside on the bed. She wasn't crying but she was petrified. She said in a faint voice "We won't survive, Radha."

I was feeling the same way but I was afraid that if I said something other people would start to cry. So I kept quiet.

Three children were sleeping on the floor. I scolded Sunil *dai* and Goma *bhauju* and had the children moved towards the end of the bed where the wall was strongest. It was made of stone and mud and didn't have any windows.

I didn't see Grandma and the eldest son so I asked, "Where are *babu* and Grandma?"

Both of them slept on the ground floor and were alone down there. Oh my God, how scared they must have felt! I couldn't even imagine.

Bhanu, who had been calling me "Radha *didi*! Radha *didi*!", had crawled under the bed as soon as he entered the room and was telling us to come under there as well. Sunil *dai* and I didn't want to do that. If there was fire or a bomb blast in our house, then there was no way we would escape. Bhanu was obviously very frightened. His voice was thick as if his mouth was dry. Whether it was due to the cold or fear, he was shivering. I felt sorry for him.

"Do you need a blanket?" I asked. "No," he replied.

"Do you want some water?"

"No," he said and just stayed under the bed shivering.

Sunil *dai* was also afraid. He was sitting towards the other end of the room, looking out now and then through the window and asking "What should we do?"

Goma *bhauju* was lying on the bed, not saying a word and barely breathing. What could I say? If I had been treating a patient then I would have known what to say.

As soon as the thought of patients came into my mind, I remembered the hospital. There had been some important construction work going on there, including some new rooms. Until it was completed we were making temporary use of local resources for the operating theatre and maternity services. For the maternity services, different equipment had been taken out of storage and sterilised and I was afraid the Maoists had taken that equipment. I was determined not to leave Jumla until the work on the hospital building was complete but I was worried my plans would have to change as a result of the attack. If I died there today, then all my worries would die with me but, if I didn't die, what would happen to my plans? When would the hospital building be complete?

I began to picture all the rooms of the hospital and then I thought of the employees. That day, only Roshana Kandel was in the staff quarters. She had evening duty. Usually, when I was alone, I used to call my colleagues to come over but on that day there was no way she could have come to my place after her duty had finished because the curfew was already in place. I could have helped her finish her duty early so she could have come with me. Normally, I strictly observe the rule that the nursing staff work in three shifts but that day I had a feeling that the Maoists might attack. Therefore, for the first time, I had broken my own rule and asked Roshana to come with me. In that sense, I had become a little weak. But she didn't want to follow me. "If I go, there could be problems. I wouldn't want you to be accused of showing favouritism," she said. She was correct but who knew the Maoists would really attack that night? Otherwise, I would never have left my patients alone.

But I regretted not bringing Roshana with me. I felt very concerned for her. She had asthma and the hospital quarters weren't very secure. Had the attack led to stress which, in turn, had led to an asthma attack? Was she lying there unconscious? Or had the attackers broken down the door and entered her quarters? My mind started to move in terrible directions. Positive thoughts were impossible.

I remembered my colleagues in Kathmandu and my boss. I remembered both my friends who helped me by wishing me well and those people who had been negative and unsupportive. Faced with imminent death, no one thinks of material things. I felt I was facing imminent death and found myself remembering and thanking those who had wished me well. I also gave forgiveness to my boss with whom I had argued many times. Every person has his or her own habits. As I am very dedicated to my work, I expect the same level of dedication in others. Ultimately, I try to force other people to be like me even though I know that's impossible. When you're facing imminent death, you realise that you might have argued with people for petty reasons.

Father's face flashed into my mind. He had problems with his stomach. When I went home during my vacation, I took some medicine for him. Recently, he had had an operation for a hernia. He didn't tell me about the operation because I was far away and he thought I'd be worried. Later, he called me to say "The operation was a success."

"All your friends have finished their PhDs. How long are you going to stay in Jumla?" he asked me from time to time.

No matter how idealistic he might be, no father would really want his daughter to go and work in Jumla. I felt for him but I didn't want to return without finishing the work I had started.

"Don't worry about me, Father," I used to reply, "I'm good wherever I am."

He couldn't say anything after that. After a long breath, he would become silent.

I remembered my mother. She didn't talk a lot. She wasn't happy that I left home to come to work in Jumla. Sometimes she just said, "Why don't you stay in Chitwan and work here?"

Tears rolled down my cheeks. I felt that I hadn't brought happiness to my parents. I thought of my sisters and my brother. All of them must have been asleep by then but the next morning they would awaken to the news from Jumla. Between now and then, anything could have happened. If I was still alive the next morning, I would call them. Otherwise, that would be it for this life. I was dying without being able to pay back even a portion of the sacrifice and love my parents had bestowed on me.

Sunil *dai* and Goma *bhauju* were remembering their deities, Chandannath and Bhairavnath. I also remembered Pashupati. I prayed silently, "Oh, Lord Pashupati, you have been watching everything. Do whatever you will."

It was very difficult to pass the time. I put a torch on inside a blanket to see the time on my watch. It was only 10:45. It felt as if time was standing still. Every second seemed like a life-time.

Our house was attached to the fence of the Agriculture Office. I felt the Maoists must have been using that fence for cover. As the fence was tall, nobody would see them but voices could be heard and we could clearly hear them cocking their guns. Every four or five minutes, the firing would stop for few seconds and we would hear the person calling again "Arun! Arun!" The firing continued. It felt as if the attackers were showing no sign of stopping.

From the sound pattern and from what we could see from the window, we assumed that the attackers had targeted the CDO and the army barracks. We were peeping through the window, when we saw a big fire at the CDO. The fire was burning brightly and in its light we saws lots of people moving around.

Sunil *dai* interrupted my thoughts, "What might have happened to our CDO?"

I was startled. I had just talked with the CDO, Damodar Pant, that afternoon. I remembered his troubled face.

Looking at his face then, I had had a feeling that something bad was about to happen.

There was fierce fighting between the Maoists and the army until two in the morning. At around two, we heard the sound of a helicopter. We thought that it must be a "night vision chopper." I had read that the government had bought such choppers to fight the Maoists.

The sound of the chopper made me hope that the fighting was about to end. I had heard that the attack on Rumjatar stopped after the night vision helicopter arrived. I rejoiced a little that my life was going to be saved. But then things went wrong.

The night vision helicopter was rounding on Khalanga Bazaar. It started to shower bombs and bullets from the sky. I feared that our house would be bombed and turned to ashes. Maoists on the ground returned fire towards the helicopter.

After one hour of intense firing, the helicopter turned away. Sunil *dai* and I discussed it and concluded it must have run out of fuel.

After the chopper returned, I don't know what Sunil *dai* was thinking but he came to me and whispered, "Will we live or die today?"

Sunil *dai* had found out only two days previously that I still had all 32 of my teeth. He congratulated me and said, "All the words spoken by a person with 32 teeth come true."

"I don't know," I'd said at the time and now I said the same thing: "I don't know. Let's see what happens."

Maybe because I had all 32 teeth, he wanted to hear me say "Yes, we will live." He became gloomy after I said "I don't know" but every few minutes he kept asking me "Will we live or die?" I got irritated. It made me regret sharing my teeth story with him.

I had heard stories of Maoist attacks from my friends in Dang and Achham but I hadn't thought they would attack so relentlessly. It was getting very cold even inside the room. How could the Maoists fight in the cold outside? I was terrified by their courage.

My prolonged state of fear made to want to pee very badly. Goma *bhauju* had asked me if I wanted to pee as well when she was using the urine container in the room. Even though I wanted to, I was too shy to do it. Now, however, it was too much. I was tired both emotionally and physically. I dropped all my shame and asked, "*Bhauju*, where is the container?"

She was lying on the bed. She gestured towards the door. Sunil *dai* showed me the chamber pot that was made by cutting the top off a gallon container. I utilised the darkness and peed in the container. Who would notice me peeing when there were the sounds of gunshots and bombs outside? I wasn't shy at all. I was so full of fear there was no room for shyness or shame.

After the night vision helicopter returned, the attack resumed with a vengeance. With our ears alert to every sound, we could surmise which places were under attack. We felt a bomb blast right in the middle of the bazaar and guessed that the police station and District Development Office had been destroyed.

Just then, on the western side of the room smoke started to come in through small holes and we could see light through the cracks. A bomb had exploded on the roof of our neighbour's house. Already in a state of panic, we were now faced with a new crisis. The fire might spread to our house.

Just two days earlier, in Europe some students had died in a fire in a school. Now I thought we would be meeting the same fate. We adults might try to bear the pain but what about the children? How would they cope with a fire? It's better to die from a bullet than fire, I thought. At least life ends easily.

Even when death is certain, humans still opt for the easiest way to die.

"Before the fire gets to our house, should we jump out the window?" Sunil *dai* and Bhanu were throwing around ideas.

From the DAO to our house was flat ground. If we jumped out the window we would be easy targets for both the Maoists and the army. And then, how would the children jump?

Another idea came to me. "Let's make a hole in the floor. Then drop quilts and blankets down. After that one of the adults can jump down and we can then get the kids down one by one."

I brought up the idea but there were no tools to make a hole in the floor. The only thing we had resembling a weapon was a small knife to cut apples.

We were still thinking as the room filled with smoke. Goma *bhauju* stood up and started to secure her stored treasures, her cash and jewellery. Sunil *dai* had kept another stash of cash with him. I realised that even at the point of death some people still cared about money. After collecting all the jewellery, she woke the kids and dressed them.

In the meantime, I was starting to worry about the cash friends from Surkhet had given me as well as important documents I had left in my room. While following Sunil *dai* to his room earlier, in a rush, I had left my room open. I wasn't worried about my own things – I didn't have much – but I was concerned about things I was holding on behalf of other people.

We heard people shouting outside. "Where is the Agriculture Office?"

Their surroundings clearly didn't match the map they had brought with them of Khalanga Bazaar. They started to curse. "What kind of map have we been given? Not a single thing is right!" After that, there was the sound of people running.

Sunil *dai* and Goma *bhauju*'s minds were still focused on their cash. I got irritated and shouted, "If we live, we can earn more money."

I was convinced that to save our lives we had to dig through the floor and started scratching at it with the small knife. Even though it was a mud floor, years of use had made it so hard that the knife broke. Now there was no alternative but to face whatever tragedy was going to come, be it bomb blast, bullets or fire.

The sound of gunfire eventually waned. Bhanu got up and looked through a hole where smoke was coming in.

"Radha *didi*," he said, "The wall is thick. It will take time for the fire to get here. It will spread first to your room, then my room and only after that to this room. By that time, it will be morning and hopefully the attack will be over."

Frightened Bhanu, who had been hiding under the bed,

had said something sensible. We calmed down. Sunil *dai* took three or four gulps of cold water.

At a distance, a rooster was crowing. It was morning. I looked at my watch. It was four. Now the attackers will go away, we thought. We were hopeful.

But expectations are not always realised.

Fierce firing started again. Bullets were continuously hitting the walls of the house and the roof. At times, we heard people screaming and thought they must have been hit by bullets.

All our expectations had crumbled to ashes. The fact that the attack was continuing till the morning meant the Maoists were winning. We thought there could be no hope for the soldiers in the barracks, let alone the police. Had the Maoists captured the barracks? From what I had heard from colleagues in Achham, anything could happen after this.

The Maoists could raid every house and kidnap people. They could steal our jewellery and cash. They could even execute people.

Oh my God!

The fighting continued until 7 am.

After that, suddenly there was no sound of explosions or gunshots. We only saw people running.

The sun was out. The sun comes up early in Jumla and the days are not foggy. I collected my courage and slowly opened the door. Sunil *dai* and Goma *bhauju* were shouting from behind me but I didn't listen to them. I actually wanted to use the bathroom. I was tired of trying to hold it.

Whatever the consequence, I went out onto the verandah. I looked in all directions. The District Police Office, Education Office, Agriculture Office and the Administration Office were all burned to the ground. The airport was still on fire.

I didn't see any Maoist attackers anywhere. I looked at the barracks. Exhausted soldiers carrying guns were walking around slowly. I also saw some police officers, lethargic and as if they had lost their senses.

Blood was everywhere. In just a single night, my lovely Jumla had been burned to the ground.

But I was still alive.

This was my rebirth.

5

THE FIRST DAY

Seeing Khalanga Bazaar completely drenched in blood, I ran towards the room of Grandmother and *Thulobabu*, Sunil *dai* and Goma *bhauju* following me.

All three of us raced towards the door and opened it. We looked around. Grandma and *Thulobabu* were both fine though their faces were pale with fear.

"How did you spend the night?" I wanted to ask. But didn't. I knew the answer.

"How did you spend the night?" Grandma must've also wanted to ask. But she didn't. She knew the answer as well.

All night we had worried about Grandma and her eldest grandson but when we finally met in the morning, we had nothing to say.

We were tired and in no mood to make conversation. We looked at each other with hopeless faces.

15 November 2002

Gunshots and bombs had turned Khalanga Bazaar into a ball of fire, just like at the cremation site in Aryaghat when dozens of corpses were burnt at the same time.

Explosions could also be still heard in some places. A few people were moving hurriedly here and there. I couldn't see their faces from afar. Were they the attackers? I didn't see any civilians.

Half burnt papers from the DAO and the Revenue Office were floating in the air. One could easily see all the burnt papers on the floor of these government offices, all those important papers relating to citizens. The burnt walls had started to fall down one by one.

Our eyes started to burn because of the smoke all over the place. My body was aching, perhaps because of lack of sleep or, more likely, because of lack of sleep combined with physical and emotional trauma.

The bazaar was also silent, even though it was almost 9 am, as if everyone had died in the previous night's attack. Even birds weren't flying in the sky.

Our house was also silent. We were only speaking with our eyes. Our lips were sealed. We didn't have the energy to move and stayed in the same place. We didn't cook and no body felt hungry. We didn't know if the kids were hungry and nobody said anything. God resides in children. Although they don't understand many things, they do understand if something happening around them is a serious issue. Therefore, seeing fear in their parents' eyes, they were also afraid.

At around 9 am, a chopper came. It was an army helicopter and landed in the barracks but it didn't just land directly there like helicopters usually did. It made several circles above the barracks then slowly descended. When it took off, it flew in a similar way. There was netting on the walls of the chopper and we could see some soldiers. This was probably a combat helicopter which had brought in additional troops. The number of troops in the barracks had increased.

As the smoke started to clear, we could see the top of the control tower at the airport. By noon, it was completely clear. I felt happy. I screamed and showed my feelings to other people in the house. Why not be happy?

Slowly, people started to come out.

But the security forces wanted to keep us caged inside like birds whose wings were cut. The Maoists had kept us awake all night, now the security personnel were not letting us move. Three people in civilian dress came, shouting "We are police officers. We escaped last night's tragedy. You shouldn't come outside. A curfew is imposed. There are bodies everywhere. There are bombs and bullets. All of you, please stay inside."

I could hardly control myself when I heard this. I didn't feel it was right for them to expect us to stay imprisoned inside our houses. The Maoists had come, attacked and left a trail of ruin behind them. So why should there now be a curfew for us civilians? A curfew hadn't stopped the attack.

I was impatient. With Sunil *dai* and Goma *bhauju* telling me not to, I went outside and through the gates of the police station. There was a socket bomb right by the gate. A channel was built down the middle of the road to carry sewage. In that channel I saw a bamboo basket which the Maoists must have brought to carry their wounded. The basket looked neat. It also had a big, fancy, cushion. It was just like the baskets we taught men to make as part of the safe motherhood programme. There used to be flower pots on both sides of the gate of police station but they had been destroyed.

On the right, blood was dripping from the verandah of a house like that of goats killed during *Dashain*. On the verandah was a decapitated human head while the rest of the body was in the doorway. While in school, I thought that the bloody history of the *Kot* and *Bhandarkhal* massacres were just works of fiction. Now I realised that a beast resides inside every human and horrors could happen when that beast is unleashed.

Soldiers and police who had survived the terror of the previous night started to remove dead bodies from inside houses. They dragged the corpses outside just like children drag their toys behind them. They brought some corpses covered in bed sheets and some on stretchers. The CDO and DSP, with whom I had lunched only the day before, had not survived.

The attack, my worries about the hospital and thoughts of family filled my mind and I didn't feel like eating anything that day. Goma *bhauju* also said "I have my period" and avoided the kitchen. She had stopped observing the restrictions placed on menstruating women as a result of my continuous counsel but clearly she didn't feel up to any work that day. Her sister-in-law made the food and the children and I ate a little.

The curfew imposed by the security forces in Khalanga Bazaar was not being strictly observed. Some local politicians and prominent people started to walk around outside. The security forces didn't take much notice of them. Ordinary civilians, however, were still not seen. People like Dilli Mahat, Devilal Thapa, Tirtha Bahadur Budha and other local leaders who had stayed out of Jumla citing security concerns, came to the Khalanga Bazaar to assess the situation. I was glad to see them. They had returned to the district when it was in need. Otherwise there would be few responsible people there. There was nobody to get advice from except the CDO and some security personnel.

They were inspecting Bishnu Furniture, which was in front of our house. I went outside to listen. The house was still on fire and one of the burning pillars fell down. Everyone screamed, "We survived the night but we might get killed now!"

In the meantime, Madan Bhatta from the then Canadian International Development Agency (CIDA) arrived. His face was grim. He smiled half-heartedly and said, "Congratulations, Radha*jee*. We survived."

Then he told me his story about the previous night. At around 10 pm, the Maoists came to his house. The commander of the group looked young and gentle. One of his colleagues was little harsh though. After talking for some time, they decided to establish a temporary clinic at his house.

The house was both the residence of the employees of CIDA and the office as well. Since their programme was about to end, there were only Madan and a helper there that night.

Madan found the Maoists to be highly disciplined. They followed their commander's orders without question or hesitation.

"There was a code of not interrupting a commander who was talking or questioning orders even amongst themselves," said Madan, "One team brought back the injured and another team gave primary treatment at the clinic. They bandaged efficiently. Then another team carried the injured away to another location."

In the evening, they ran out of supplies. The commander asked Madan for some clothe that could be used as a bandage. Madan tore a piece of bed sheet and handed it to him. They asked for hot water. He game them water from a thermos flask. They then asked detailed questions about his office. Who were the people working there and what did they do? In the morning, before leaving they asked for money. After the rumour of an impending attack in Jumla, none of the organisations, including CIDA, kept any spare cash for fear of getting robbed.

"I don't have any cash," Madan said. He had spent all the money he had the previous day. They didn't believe him and became insistent.

"If you don't have money from your employer, then give us your own money," they said.

Madan took out his wallet and showed it to them. He had only two thousand rupees. "Take one thousand and leave one thousand for me," he said.

At first they didn't agree and wanted to take all the money until one Maoist felt pity for him and said, "It's okay. Leave him." So they didn't take any of his money and his two thousand rupees was saved.

They stayed all night with him, running their clinic in his

home. When they were leaving, however, they turned on him and threatened to burn his house down.

At that time, there was cross-fire outside. A bomb dropped from the night vision helicopter was shaking the house. But Madan said, "Those young fighters just kept on working confidently, despite their age. They didn't panic at all even when the helicopter came. Instead they were shouting at it: For how long can you drop bombs? You will have to return sooner or later when you run out of gasoline."

The most astonishing thing was, even though they had captured his house, they were still giving him suggestions on how to stay safe. They showed him a way to go to his neighbour's house. His next door neighbour was Lal Bahadur Thapa, who worked in the Rastriya Banijya Bank. Just as the Maoists suggested, Madan took out his important belongings and went to his neighbour's house amidst all the shooting and bombing.

"I reached his house but how to get the door open?" he said. "Nobody opened the door, however many times I tried. They had to come outside to open the door and who would do that?"

After Madan shouted a few times "It's me. Open the door!" Thapa's wife finally opened the door.

After Madan was gone, the Maoists dragged out his mattress and blankets. Then they planted a bomb in his house and blew it up.

"Thank God my life was saved," said Madan with a deep breath.

Madan was full of praise for the commander because he had spared his life. He said "If their commander is a gentlemen, then they will spare civilians" at least 10 times.

In Tundikhel, 46 dead bodies were lined up.

The CDO, four soldiers, 20 police, 19 Maoists, and two local civilians had died in the attack. We found out later that one staff member from the Revenue Office had also been killed. The dead bodies of the Maoists were placed in one row and the rest in another row. The body of DSP Bijeshwor Ghimire was never found.

DSP Mandal's body was there. I had treated him once. He had come to the hospital for gastritis. There were no doctors so I attended to him. The pain was so intense he was in tears. At that time he said, "I'm working just so my children can complete their studies. Otherwise I would have left already." His children were studying medicine and engineering. I gave him medicine and his condition improved.

Now his lifeless body was lying there in front of me.

The Maoists had attacked the prison at around 9:15 pm. The prison was in a sloping area far from Khalanga Bazaar and near the river. An explosion there wouldn't be heard very clearly in the bazaar. The sound that we heard during dinner was that blast which, at the time, we just accepted as normal. The Maoists bombed the prison, captured it and took some walkie-talkie sets. All the prisoners were set free.

After that, they attacked the DAO, army barracks and the district police office. When the police said that they couldn't fight anymore, the army had called DSP Bijeswor Ghimire to come to the barracks. He was instructed to come using an alternative route through the Science Education Training Hall, however, the Maoists got this information via the stolen walkie-talkies and laid a trap for him there.

Then they surrounded the police station. The Maoists were crawling uphill to reach it.

On the other side, another team of Maoists started to cut the wires on the mine which had been planted in front of the barracks. They killed some soldiers who were standing guard. But then the army shot the attackers who were trying to cut the wires. "Good action" was taken by the army. At least they were able to save the barracks. Only four soldiers on the frontline were killed.

We were all anxious to find out which civilians had lost their lives.

Seeing the bodies, we recognised a mentally retarded person who lived near the Kalikholi rivulet on the way to the airport. Another man was killed when he was looking out his window. The Maoists did not want to kill civilians. The military had also not counter-attacked as strongly as they could have because they also wanted to keep civilians safe. Had they fought to win, they could have certainly won.

It was easier to counter the Maoist attack from the barracks which was situated at a height instead of coming out onto flat land. Had they done that, however, it might have put civilian lives at greater risk. Since the houses were made of pinewood, if the Maoists set fire to one of the houses, then all houses could be on fire in no time.

I went to the hospital, hearing different stories from different people on the way. As usual I was going through Science Education Training Hall. Bullet casings were all over the road as well as socket bombs. We had to be very careful to avoid these while walking. There was not a single house that did not have bullet holes. This gave a clear picture of the intensity of the attack.

On the way, I met Roshana. I was relieved to see her. The poor girl had been alone in the hospital quarters all night. Early in the morning she had gone to *Subba* Jit Bahadur KC and cried. However, she did not show any tears to me and I didn't want to reopen her wounds.

I met some friends from International Nepal Fellowship (INF) who had come there to upgrade Jumla hospital. Narayan from INF showed me his office. The Maoists had entered the building by breaking the lock on the gate. In Jumla, most of the houses had doors and windows made of pinewood, which was not very hard to break.

The Maoists had also broken open a cupboard that was used to store the handicrafts made by people with leprosy which were now scattered on the floor. They had also packed up the computer in readiness for taking it but hadn't. There was money in the safe which they also hadn't taken.

INF treats mostly leprosy patients.

The Maoists put all the patients in a single room. They emptied another room to use as a treatment centre for their injured. The floor of that room was awash with blood. Everything they had used that night – saline, pipes and swabs – had been left behind. The saline they used was unusual. I had never seen a bottle of that type in the operating theatre of Bir Hospital. They had eaten corn, soybeans, biscuits and noodles when they were there. Bits and pieces were scattered around.

They had also been to the INF staff quarters. They said, "There must be people inside. Otherwise we would have blown it up." After saying that, they knocked on the door.

Up until then, my friends from INF had been laying low upstairs holding their breath. They heard what the Maoists said outside. The wife of one of the staff members who stayed on the ground floor opened the door

"Who's inside?" they asked.

"We are only staff members here," she said.

"It's cold outside. Do you have any warm clothes?"

She pointed towards three children sleeping on the floor and said, "Those kids are using some blankets. If you want, I can give them to you."

After seeing the children, one of them said, "We are fighting for their future. We won't take their blankets."

After listening to the talk of my friends from INF, I went to the hospital. There was no staff. Krishna and Ganga were on night duty. I started to look around different parts of the hospital with Tara.

The door of the Emergency Unit was wide open and they had broken into all cupboards. Aprons used by doctors and nurses during operations were scattered everywhere. Packs that were sterilised were open. However, it may not have been only the Maoists who were looking for things to steal. In only 18 months there, I had come to understand that not all the staff was honourable or well-intentioned.

The Maoists had also treated their wounded comrades in the Emergency Room. It was said they had their own doctor, however, they also forced another doctor to come to the hospital. It was only when they were on the way, that they realised that he was a veterinarian. Once they reached the hospital quarters, he said, "Listen, I'm a veterinarian. The doctor for humans lives here."

Then the Maoists went to take the doctor as well.

Dr. Pannalal Shah was always frightened. Staff didn't like his sullen attitude. The previous night he had been petrified. He said, "Sister, there might be an attack today, have you heard?"

"There are attacks here every day, doctor," I teased.

It took quite some time for Shah to come out of his quarters. People were joking that it must have taken him an hour to reach the hospital because in order to escape the bullets and bombs he crawled all the way on his hands and knees. After taking him to the hospital, the Maoists made him sit on a chair and did all the work themselves.

After seeing his face, one of the Maoists asked, "Doctor, are you afraid?"

When he didn't reply, the fighter said, "Don't worry. I'll save you, even if it means standing in the way of a bullet."

In the meantime, another team brought the acting head of the Public Service Commission, Prem Prasad Acharya, from his quarters.

The Maoists entered Prem's room and after interrogating him for some time, they said, "All right, now pack your things."

He wanted to pack some books but they scolded him and took his bag, shoes and socks. They also took his camera. He said, "That camera isn't mine. It belongs to a friend." They laughed at him. "Can't we take your friend's things?"

They also asked for his jacket. Prem only had one jacket which he was wearing. When he started to take it off, they said "It's okay. Don't take off the jacket you're wearing."

We moved forward while talking and reached the hospital store room. The Maoists had created a mess in there. It had taken me three full days to clean the dust out and organise materials required for emergencies, operations and maternal health care. I had arranged and labelled everything. There were also some stretchers and instruments to measure blood pressure in the store room but they were gone. Was it done by the Maoists or by somebody else?

In the meantime, identified bodies were brought to the hospital for post-mortems. A large number of people were gathered outside the mortuary. Families and relatives of the deceased were crying. Some were screaming.

Until then, we staff who were not locals hadn't contacted our families. The news of the Jumla attack must have been broadcasted on the TV and radio by that time and I realised my family must be very worried about me. I was agitated. I had to let them know that I was alive at any cost. The telephone line was cut so there was no way I could use it. I wanted to use the security coordinator's satellite phone but it was also not working. He advised me to use the satellite phone in the army barracks instead.

We went toward the barracks avoiding bullets and socket bombs on the way.

We sent a message to Major Hiraman Joshi through one of the security guards at the gate. I had met him before. Since I had started to build a new hospital building, many people recognised me. Also I was the only female officer in the district. The Major easily gave his time to us.

His voice was totally hoarse and he looked exhausted but he was smiling. We congratulated him on being successful in protecting the barracks. He said, "Thanks." After some talk about the attack, we asked his permission to use his satellite phone to call to our families and he readily agreed.

We gave him our families' names and telephone numbers and he promised he would notify all our homes. Whether he did or not, I don't know.

In the barracks, I met Inspector Amar Bam and his wife, Bishnu. We congratulated each other for being alive. It was one of those times when you had to be happy just to be alive and be congratulated for being safe.

"At around eleven last night, I saw the DAO burning and I was worried you might be inside," I said, "Thank God, you're safe." They said much the same thing to me.

I had known both Amar and his wife from the hospital where they came to get treatment for Bishnu. Whenever a doctor was not available and some VIPs were to be treated, I used to be called on. Their home was in Mahendranagar. Bishnu's parents lived in Bhairahawa. Her husband hadn't got any leave for a long time, so she had sent their children to live in a hostel and had come to live in Jumla.

After the Maoists attacked the DAO, they escaped from their home to Bhagawati Shrestha's house. "Bhagawati's sister recognised our voices and immediately opened the door," said Bishnu, tears flowing down her face. "Otherwise we wouldn't be meeting you today!"

For the first time in my life, I was totally elated to meet and speak to people. I felt as if I were meeting them again after many years' separation. All the meetings that day were special because they were our first meetings returning safely from the road to death. Life is just a collection of moments lived between chances. There is nothing we can take with us. We get nothing by getting angry with others, feeling low or arguing. That just gives us things to regret on our deathbed.

After meeting the Bam couple I went straight to Tundikhel.

The crowd was increasing. There were many journalists. I hoped that if there were some journalists that I knew, I could get a message to my family. I tried to get into the crowd. If I got captured in a photo then there might be a possibility that I would be seen in the newspaper or on TV and my family would know I was alive. But my efforts were futile. I was too late.

I felt lost and disappointed and returned home across the bridge over the Jugaad River. On the way was the Science Education Training Hall. It was badly damaged. The smoke was still rising. There was a pool of blood at the front. A policeman was searching for something.

"What are you looking for?" I asked.

"DSP Bijeshwor was killed here," he said, "I'm looking to see if I can find any proof."

I also started to search among the ruins. I saw a small chunk of something that had been burned. I picked it up with the help of a sheet of white plastic. It was a human bone, probably from the spine.

"This must be a bone belonging to the DSP," he said.

"How do you know?" I asked.

"We found a piece of his belt and the shoes that he was wearing."

I couldn't speak when I heard this. I just stared at him. Then he went towards Tundikhel and I returned home via the District Police office.

Finding a piece of DSP Bijeshwor's body disturbed me deeply. He had said on his walkie-talkie, "I am coming via the Basanti Hotel." After hearing that, the Maoists had targeted him and bombed the Science Education Building.

He was a nice-looking man who spoke very well. "I'm a classmate of Baburam Bhattarai," he used to say. He sometimes drank beer early in the morning, perhaps because of the pressure of his job. As I stayed in the hotel, I somehow knew the eating and drinking habits of most of the VIPs in Jumla.

There was a decree from the Home Ministry not to give leave to any security personnel during the State of Emergency. Therefore, DSP Bijeshwor had stayed in Jumla even during *Dashain* and *Tihar*. His daughter had come to visit him only the previous last week. The last time I met him, he was thinking about his daughter. That was their last meeting.

When I reached home, Sunil *dai* and Madan had more news. The Maoists had stolen noodles, biscuits, clothes, blankets and shoes from all houses that were to the west of our hotel.

Why did they spare us? We started to wonder. Maybe it was because our house was the first house after the bazaar. Or maybe it was because there was a clear view of our house from the barracks? Another possibility presented itself. It all depended on who their commander was. Maoist leaders like Parbat, Angad and Naresh knew us well. Were we spared on their orders?

It was getting dark. In Jumla, the high hills start to block the sun from two in the afternoon. It feels that evening comes very fast. It was also very cold. We started to make a fire. Just then, we heard a loud knock on the door. It was Gorakh Bahadur Kau whom we called "Uncle". He started to cry loudly. I was speechless to see an adult like him crying. We were all baffled. Did something happen at his house, was someone killed, was his house burned down or robbed?

The Maoists hadn't let Uncle Gorakh stay in his home for a long time so he stayed with us and sometimes he went to his home in secret. His family shared *tika* on *Dashain* and *Tihar* with Sunil *dai*'s family.

Seeing the condition he was in, we couldn't speak. We just stared at each other. Finally, I gathered some courage and asked, "What happened? Did the Maoists do something to your house?"

"These are tears of joy," he said. "Last night, I thought I would never see anyone again. I'm crying with happiness to see everyone safe."

Poor Uncle. It turned out the Maoists had tortured him all night.

He had been to his sister's house that night. His brother-in-law, Tirtha Bahadur Budha, was the President of the District Development Committee. The Maoists came to the house and began interrogating Gorakh, asking "Where is your brother-in-law? Take us to him."

"I'm only a visitor. I just got here myself. I don't know anything" he said, begging with his hands together.

After nothing worked to make him reveal where Tirtha

was, one of the Maoists said, "In that case, you have to show us the houses of the people listed on this piece of paper."

To save his own life, Gorakh had no alternative. All night long, he walked with the Maoists to show them the houses. For some people, he said, "I don't recognise that name." They made him walk until four in the morning. They released him only after reaching the bottom of the road going towards Kalikot.

"I came straight here," he said.

His tears were both because he was happy to see us alive and because he was happy to be alive. However, I'm sure he also regretted having been compelled to show the Maoists the houses of the people on their list.

We were hearing many different stories. There was an overseer from Tanahun whose posting was in the Jumla District Office. He had come to Jumla just to process paperwork for his study leave. In the night he stayed in a guest house. He was alone in a new place and, in addition to that, the Maoists were attacking. He was petrified and stayed under the bed all night.

We also heard of some lucky people who had left Jumla the day before the attack, including Gauri Bahadur, brother of pilot Anil Karki who had flown the army chopper, who was a judge in the Appellate Court, and Local Development Officer, Hari Bashistha.

Then another rumour took hold: the Maoists were planning to attack again! Their aim was to capture the barracks but that goal had not been fulfilled due to geographical issues. The map they had brought with them was too inaccurate.

We also heard more stories about the affect the attack had on the Maoists. It was said that in Jumla the Maoists had to fight longer than usual and had sustained a lot of casualties. They were still lurking around in neighbouring villages, hiding in various houses and might attack again at an opportune time.

Amidst this speculation, people coming from districts outside of Jumla were in a hurry to get out of the war zone and return home. Even though they had survived, the concern of their family members made them not to care about their jobs.

But what about the Jumlis? Where could they go? They were born and raised in Jumla. How could they leave their ancestral home because the security situation was unstable?

When there is no alternative to fear, we long for only one thing – courage.

We planned to eat early and then sleep. Everyone from the family lay down in the same room. The children and Sunil *dai* slept on the bed. Goma *bhauju*, Grandma, the eldest son and me slept on the floor.

There was no light in the room. I didn't have the will to light the *tuki*. We didn't even want to speak. We just stared at the ceiling. Who knew if we would have to wake up to the sound of bullets and bombs again?

We didn't know when we dozed off.

6

THE SECOND DAY

16 November 2002

Bishwaraj Bhatta, a survivor of the Accham attack, worked in my office in Kailali. He had briefed us about the Maoist attack in Mangalsen. "Until you are personally affected, you think the security policy is sound and straightforward," said he. "But once you have been affected, it's very difficult to work."

In the security policy, it stated that officers should be rescued from a war zone as soon as possible, however, putting that policy into effect was not an easy process. He said, "It takes a long time to obtain the necessary permissions from the airport and the Home Ministry." After hearing his words, I had no faith that a chopper would immediately come to rescue us. I was quite hopeful on the second day though. Would it come without any prior notice?

If there had been no attack, I would have already reached Surkhet. There was a follow up programme about prevention of infection. Madan from CIDA had wanted to go with me. He had planned to go on to New Delhi today. He was held up due to some administrative work and distributing paycheques to his staff.

Madan came to me early in the morning. We talked about security issues. "Security personnel from our office are planning to rescue you as well," he said, "They must have already coordinated it. Otherwise we will go down together."

His idea was that if we could go down from Jumla, we could make some financial arrangements in Surkhet or Nepalganj.

After talking with Madan, I changed my dress and walked towards the airport. I already had packed all my things two days ago.

Smoke was still coming from the DAO. Walls of houses were falling one after another. The second day after the attack, the bazaar was still quiet. It was midday but it was as silent as night. There were no children on the road. There were shops, doors open, robbed by the Maoists. According to locals, the Maoists searched for policemen in every house. The Maoists had adopted a policy to search and then kidnap or kill policemen, said the villagers.

Jumla was completely changed. Nobody trusted anyone. But still we were obliged to trust. Even though our hearts were aching, we had to face the world and smile. In the past, we could see lots of police guarding the DAO. There was nobody there that day. Nobody stopped us. I remembered the face of the CDO Damodar Pant and became emotional.

I walked towards the Chandannath temple to get some peace of mind. There was not a single sign of conflict at the temple. There were small huts next to the temple where the priests lived and all of those were intact. So many people had died in the bazaar. Twenty-eight official buildings were burned. There was millions of rupees worth of damage. Both the living and those who died might have called upon and prayed to Chandannath. Their prayers weren't answered but there was no damage to the temple.

The police station opposite the temple was in ruins however. The shiny ceramic pots, neat garden, clean house and uniformed police were all gone. They were just memories now. The pavement was stained with blood. It looked like a ghost house.

Near the statue outside the DAO, I saw a security guard in civilian dress. I went near him and greeted him, "*Namaste*". He returned the gesture of greeting but didn't speak.

To break the ice, I asked him a question, "Were you with the CDO that night?"

It turned out he was looking for someone to share his feelings with and started to tell me all the details. "We only realised they were attacking when they started to surround the office. Our colleagues were firing from the police station. I pleaded with the boss, 'We can't withstand this attack. We should run'. He was anxious. He was worried about what to do next. I begged him again, 'Let's get out of here now' but he said, 'You guys go. I'll stay in the bunker', and then he went into the bunker."

These bunkers had been constructed after rumours of an impending attack on Jumla started to intensify. I had never even heard the term "bunker" before that.

The CDO's bodyguard continued his story. "The Maoists

bombed our office between 10:30 pm and 10:45 pm. I believe he died from suffocation in the bunker."

"Wasn't he shot in the eye?" I asked. "How could he run after he had been shot?"

The bodyguard continued "When I left him in the bunker and came out, there were lots of Maoists on the lawn in front of the office. My colleague and I started to run between the houses. My colleague was shot from behind. He started screaming, "Ah! I'm dying. Water! Water!" I had lost all my senses but I was still moving forward. Then I came across another group of Maoists."

I was fascinated by his story.

"That group asked, 'Who are you?' I remembered I had heard somebody use the name 'Kishan Comrade' some time back. I prayed to God, and said 'Kishan Comrade'. As it turned out, they didn't know all of their comrades. 'It's okay' they said and they went their own way."

Having survived being prey to the Maoists, he went to a nearby house. He banged on the door very loudly. At first nobody came to open the door. After he continuously banged on the door, one very frightened guy came to open it. And then he saved his life by staying in that house for the whole night.

He was very emotional as he shared his story. Tears were welling in his eyes. If the talk continued for much longer, they would have flowed down his face.

"Everything is burnt to ashes." He pointed to the District Administration Office. "And I don't even want to look over there."

Thinking about the CDO, I told myself I would remember his bodyguard's story and went towards the airport.

The District Education Office was on the way. It was also burnt to the ground. Some of the neighbouring houses were also burnt, damaged or destroyed. Up the slope were the quarters of Deepak, the Airport Tower Chief, and a guesthouse. Both had been burned to the ground.

It hadn't been all that long since the control tower at the airport was inaugurated. The new airport was targeted by the Maoists before it could help Jumla transform. The wall of the tower was dotted with bullet holes. The frames of the door and the windows were burnt. Pieces of broken glasses were everywhere. Smoke had changed the colour of the building from yellow to black.

I wanted to meet Deepak. He lived in Jumla with his wife and son. I walked up to the tower with him.

"For today I can't say, but tomorrow a plane might come," he said. "The army must be communicating."

A pressure cooker bomb was used to blow up the tower. The handle of the cooker was found there. Some socket bombs were also found.

"The airport was only attacked in the morning," I said, "I was looking from my house and I could see it burning."

Deepak started sharing his experiences.

That night, a group of Maoists came to the airport at about 10 pm. "There will be an attack tomorrow," they said. "We will not spare anything, even the tower. But we won't harm you. We will come in the morning."

All night the combat continued. As dawn was breaking

and the Maoists hadn't come, the airport staff was happy believing the tower would be saved. Just then they heard the voices of two girls. "Leave the building. We are going to bomb this place," they said.

Deepak left without arguing. Then the tower was blown up.

While Deepak was sharing his story, some men came towards us, shouting. Their voices were not distinct as all of them were yelling at the same time. It turned out they had found a bomb and were running away in fear it might explode.

On the other side of the airport was the office of Salt Trading and Nepal Food Corporation. According to some villagers, the night after the attack the Maoists had come again. There was a rumour that they had stolen some food so I went there to confirm the facts.

It turned out to be just a rumour.

Attacks and rumours went hand in hand. It was understood that it was a Maoist tactic to attack after spreading destabilising rumours. There was a big rumour that the Maoists were going to lure choppers coming from Surkhet and Nepalganj and then hijack them. There were also rumours that the Maoists would distribute free food looted from Nepal Food Corporation.

I was hearing lots of stories.

Since there was no way a plane was leaving that day, I returned to the hospital and comforted my friends. I promised them that, if by any luck I reached Surkhet, I would send messages to all their families. I was feeling lost thinking about my own family and the dreadful situation of Jumla. I felt restless and couldn't stay indoors.

I went towards the Agriculture Office. The buildings of the Agriculture Development Bank and the Agriculture Research Centre were in ruins. There was a smell of burnt wheat. During my childhood, I had seen two houses burn. At that time, charred wood and burns on the backs of some buffaloes left a really bad impression of fire on my young brain. But this was so much worse.

There was a tractor on the lawn of the Agriculture Office that had also been burned. I hadn't been to the Agriculture Office before. I didn't have to go there for any professional reason. It was also a little far. However, I used to interact with its staff at the CDO's monthly meetings.

Now after the Maoist attack, all of us were on the same page. I saw some of the staff there and felt no hesitation in talking to them. I slowly walked towards them.

One of them told me he had felt safer to stay outside during the attack. He climbed a pine tree and stayed there all night. "As far as my eyes could see, there were Maoists everywhere," he said. "I can't say exactly how many but wherever I looked, they were there. Perhaps there were 10,000 of them."

It is very tough to stay outside in the freezing cold of Jumla. In addition to this, the night vision helicopter was continuously showering down rockets and bullets. "I don't know how I survived," he said.

I was appalled to hear his story. I stood up and without speaking a word, went towards Madan's room. His office was completely burnt. An unexploded bomb, probably thrown from the night vision chopper, was stuck in the ground.

From there, I walked towards the Telecommunications Office. There were only ruins left. I had heard that a new system had been introduced there in the last few days whereby we could make an appointment to make a telephone call. It took at least two hours to make a single successful call from Jumla. The Maoists must have known about this new technology because they destroyed only the old building.

I heard a couple crying loudly near the district police office. Every day on the way to my office, I used to see the couple in that house although I had never spoken to them and I was curious to know why they were crying like that on the second day after the attack. I asked other people nearby.

"The Maoists beat them because their son has joined the police force," they told me. The Maoists tortured not only people who were employed in the police force but their relatives as well.

As the morning came, the Maoists looked more stressed. Was it because of hunger or the fact that they knew they couldn't win that made them gulp water a lot even in that cold? They ate apples very quickly. They searched for and took any shoes they could find. Whichever homes they went into, they exchanged their old shoes for newer ones.

As I was strolling in the village, I saw Babukaji Silwal, the manager of the Rastriya Banijya Bank sitting next to the fireplace, looking despondent. I was aware that the bank had been bombed but I wanted to hear about the incident in his own words.

The bank was in a building rented from a local businessman, Dharma Raj Rawal, in the middle of Tundikhel and close to the barracks. On the top floor of the same building was

Silwal's quarters. Because of security concerns, he was not able to go home even during *Dashain* and *Tihar*. His wife had come to Jumla during her *Dashain* holidays. At around 10 pm that night, he said to the guard, "Stay on your toes. There was shooting today. We might be attacked."

Then he went upstairs and started listening to the news. He had a habit of updating himself on the security status of the day with the news at 11 pm.

While he was listening to the news, somebody knocked on the door. "Who is it?" he asked in his regular stern voice.

In reply, a group of Maoists kicked down the door and entered his room. "Don't you know who we are?" they said, pointing guns at both sides of his head, "Show us the safe."

Silwal trembled. Before he could even think, they said, "Show us the cash balance."

"The balance is with the cashier," said he, joining both his hands.

"Where does the cashier live?" a loud voice yelled.

Before he could reply, another Maoist had already brought the keys from the cashier. "Open the safe," said, giving the keys to Silwal but his hands were shaking so badly that he couldn't open the lock. One of the Maoists said, "In Sandhikharka we broke the safe open by kicking it. Why do we need keys here?"

They used bayonets and their feet to break into the safe. Including used and unused bills, there were Rs 1.4 million inside. They wrapped all the cash in a cloth. Some of them then hit Silwal, asked for more money and threatened to kill him.

"He must have hidden it in the barracks," one man said and started kicking Silwal.

In the crowd of Maoists, there was one woman. Silwal turned towards her, tremblingly, put both his hands together and begged, "Please, Sister, that's all the money I have. Since it was pay-day in all the offices, most of the money is gone. I have a daughter like you. I'm only working here for her."

The woman must have taken pity on him and stopped her comrades from assaulting him anymore. Then she started the detonation of a pressure cooker bomb.

The Maoists who had come to rob the bank must have been very hungry. They ate all the biscuits in the room. They even offered a few to Silwal.

"I don't want anything to eat," he said.

"Can't you eat what we give you? Have we poisoned it?" they growled.

They asked for water after finishing the biscuits.

"There is no drinking water here," he said helplessly.

"You won't even give us water?" they shouted at him.

Silwal's mouth was dry due to fear and cold, as well as the biscuit the Maoists had made him to eat. He dropped a second biscuit to the floor without them noticing.

After preparing the bomb, the attackers left the house, taking Silwal with them. They started to pour an accelerant around the house though Silwal couldn't tell if it was kerosene or diesel.

"They burned the building down in front of my eyes," said Silwal in a dying voice, "I was afraid they might also burn me or kidnap me."

But they didn't do anything like that. Instead, they locked him in a nearby building which was still under construction. The bomb exploded only a minute or two after they left.

"When the bomb went off, the house I was locked in was shaking. I was worried the fire might spread to that building as well," he said, "I thought all night of God and my family."

In the morning when everything was calm, he managed to get out. He didn't have any clothes or possessions. Everything had been burned along with the bank. He asked some friends for clothes and was wearing a jacket provided by his landlord, Dharma Raj. Silwal was a little short and Dharma Raj's jacket didn't fit him very well. Dharma Raj had brought a pair of shoes from a nearby store. Sunil *dai* chose his own pants. I don't know if they fitted him at the waist but they were far too long and folded over two or three times at the bottom.

Listening to stories of the attack all day made me sad. I kept thinking about my family.

The silence in Khalanga Bazaar was still there. We didn't hear the sounds of bombs and gunshots like previous days. Dogs, chickens and wild animals must have been frightened by the attack. We didn't hear any barking, clucking or screeching.

I was also struck dumb. Not only could I not speak but my brain felt numb.

In the evening, all of us slept in the same room again, staring at the ceiling.

We didn't know when we fell asleep.

7

THE THIRD DAY

17 November 2002

A few ladies were washing clothes in the Jugaad River and a small number of shops had opened. Children had started to play on the road again. They had started to run. In teashops, there was hot discussion about politics and the conflict, along with hot cups of tea.

Jumla had started to come alive again.

I went to the hospital as usual and comforted my friends, promising I would call their families as soon as I reached Nepalganj or Surkhet. I didn't know whether I would be able to go or not. I was thinking I would go by whatever means I could. I didn't even have to reach my home. I would be satisfied just to speak to my family on the phone.

I went to the airport. The army had started to take pictures and assess the damage. I returned home. There were four cows lying dead in a field. Those cows were from the Chandannath temple.

People were saying there were lots of human remains along the banks of the Tila River. Some bodies were buried; some were just thrown on the ground. Dogs had started to mangle the bodies. Many of the dead were very young, little more than children. Some bodies were in uniform and some were in civilian dress. We heard news that the body of a female commander was also found. Along with the body, they found a diary in which the preparations for the attack had been written in code.

However hard people tried to get back to normal life, news of this sort disturbed everyone deeply. Employees and businessman were ready to go to Surkhet or Nepalganj as soon as possible. Everyone was waiting for a plane but the only things in the sky were military choppers.

All of a sudden, a white helicopter appeared and started to make circles over Khalanga Bazaar. I kept looking. Slowly it landed in the barracks. My eyes were riveted to it. A new helicopter in Jumla led to lots of speculation. Some said there were more soldiers killed in the attack than had been publicly acknowledged and the helicopter had come to take those bodies away in secret.

I started to wonder. To show that the security policy was being implemented, DFID and my office should have sent a chopper to pick me up. But then again, I thought, if they were going to evacuate me there were other alternatives. Why should they send a helicopter?

I was looking at the chopper from the front of my house. I saw that a child was running towards my home with a small piece of paper in his hand.

"Which is the Everest Hotel?" he asked.

The words "This is it," came into my brain but I controlled myself. I thought that I shouldn't divulge any information without knowing who he was and why he had come there.

He spoke as if he had heard the voice in my mind, "Somebody called Radha Paudel lives here. The pilot of the helicopter that landed in the barracks wants her to come."

Now I was sure. The helicopter had come to pick me up. My mind started to become animated. I was very anxious to meet my father or hear the voice of my mother. Hurriedly I told everyone in the house that I was leaving. They also became happy. They brought out the bag that I had packed in readiness. Sunil *dai* wanted to come up to the barracks. He wanted to see me off and I didn't object.

We went straight to the barracks. I gave my details to the security guard. He didn't believe me at first and wouldn't let me in. I looked around to see if I could find someone I knew but I didn't find anyone. I asked the disbelieving guard, "Could you please inform the pilot that Radha Paudel is here?"

Just then, I saw the Administration Head of my office, Krishna Sharma, coming down the steps of the barrack. He had come personally to pick me up. Krishna Sharma was the same person who, during my interview for employment with the safe motherhood programme had asked me "Between Jumla and Nawalparasi, which place do you want to go?"

I greeted him, "*Namaste*!"

He didn't return my greeting but hugged me with one arm and asked, "What's up, *Bunu*?"

Because I was younger than the others, most of the people in the Kathmandu office called me "*Bunu*", a Nepali term for younger sister. Since Krishna himself had come in the helicopter, we didn't talk about general security policy but we did talk about why it took so long for the helicopter to come and I told him who should return in the helicopter with us.

I said that we should take Dr. Shah, friends from INF and Madan from CIDA. He showed me a letter from DFID which said that I alone should be evacuated and said, "We can't take anyone else."

I felt sad but Madan had come to the barracks and I noticed he was smiling. And he was not carrying a bag.

I bid goodbye to everyone. Sunil *dai*'s eyes were filled with tears as we waved goodbye. The door of the helicopter closed. The blades started to rotate and slowly we rose into the air.

Goodbye army barracks, burnt government buildings, burnt and demolished private homes, deserted Khalanga Bazaar and Everest Hotel, where I had found a home and a family.

Who says a hotel can't be a home? Sunil *dai* and Goma *bhauju*'s hotel was more than a home to me. I was born in my home but I was reborn in the Everest Hotel.

The helicopter ascended rapidly. The entire Jumla valley was spread out in front of me, benighted as it was by poverty, lack of education, inequality and conflict. How long would these afflictions torment Jumla? Why couldn't someone find a cure?

I am a nurse but that was way beyond my capabilities otherwise I would have healed Jumla then and there. Its pain was my pain as well. Poor Jumla, I thought. It seems the medicine to heal your afflictions can't be found in this country. Where can we find it?

Hills and forests started to disappear behind the clouds. The meandering rivers, like the part in my mother's hair, were no longer visible. My mother still parts her hair like that. My vision started to become blurry. I blinked my eyes to remove any dirt but still my eyesight didn't become clear.

I had first landed in Jumla in a helicopter that carried drums of coal tar and other things. I had become so used to the difficult life in Jumla that the four-seater helicopter of Karnali Air felt new and strange to me. Leaving Jumla after that long, black night made me feel happy yet some part of me was already missing it.

I was getting tears in my eyes at the thought of seeing my family again while, at the same time, I wanted to cry because I was leaving Jumla at such a critical time.

The helicopter was slowly descending.

As the helicopter landed, I became emotional. I had endured threats from the Maoists or people pretending to be Maoists. I had grappled with bureaucracy. I had seen many patients close-up. Death had become normal for me. Many people had died in front of my eyes. Then I had spent a whole night in the middle of a raging battle. I had comforted Sunil *dai*, Goma *bhauju* and their children.

For two days, I had searched, trying to understand the point of the war. I believe I am strong, lion-hearted even. Other people say the same thing about me. But, that day, sitting in that helicopter, I felt weak and exhausted.

As every second went by, I felt as if my soul was leaving my body. I felt like I was dying. Why? I don't know exactly.

The helicopter landed at Nepalganj airport.

Khila Ojha from the administration section of my organisation ran towards me across the tarmac and hugged me saying "*Bunu!*" But I couldn't react, not because I didn't want to but because no reaction came to my mind.

I don't know why.

I just smiled.

When we reached the airport gates, I heard that our National Programme Director, Susane Klafam, wanted to talk to me. I didn't want to talk to anyone. I wanted to ignore them all and say "I'll call her tomorrow."

I don't know why.

Just to keep her happy, I spoke with her.

At that time, I wanted to cry out loud. It felt as if a volcano was erupting inside me and all I wanted to do was burst into tears. But I controlled myself.

I called home but didn't have the courage to speak frankly.

I don't know why.

"First you talk for some time, then I'll talk" I said to Khila and he responded accordingly.

After some time I spoke with my sister. She was very angry but it was anger born of love. She started to ask questions about my accommodation and my office.

I didn't have a lot of energy to talk so I cut our conversation short.

"I'm coming to Kathmandu tomorrow," I said, "So I'll be home the day after tomorrow."

Before putting down the phone, I said, "I want to hear Mother's voice."

She gave the phone to Mother. She had been waiting to talk with me. As soon as she grabbed the receiver she said, "We were so worried..."

I couldn't control myself when I heard her voice. I immediately hung up the phone.

Why? I don't know...

8

HOME ON THE FIFTH DAY

I kept my promise.

I called the homes of all my friends in the hospital and informed their children, parents and family members that they were alive.

After spending a night in Nepalganj, our team reached the airport early in the morning of 18 November. It took almost an hour and half to reach Kathmandu in the helicopter.

Friends from the office had come to meet me at the airport. Everyone was happy to see me alive. Saraswoti Chhetri hugged me as soon as she saw me. She couldn't hold back her tears. She left the room and started sobbing. She is very soft-hearted and we were very close when I worked in the Kathmandu office before I went to Jumla.

That day Susane said she wanted to take me to her home. I was not interested but I didn't want to hurt her feelings. After facing death and surviving, my heart was wider than the sky, accommodating everyone.

I went to her house.

I found everything in Kathmandu new and strange, as if I were experiencing it for the first time. The newness didn't attract me. I felt like an alien who had suddenly arrived on planet Earth. I felt like a stranger in a strange land.

My chest felt heavy, as if I were being crushed by a great weight. I felt very isolated and called home again.

"I'm coming home tomorrow."

I didn't want to talk for a long time. They wanted to meet me at the airport but I didn't want them to.

I said, "The flight times are very unreliable. I don't know when I'll land."

My sister must have been surprised to hear the way I spoke, without any excitement. My voice sounded foreign even to me.

19 November 2002

I had prepared thank you cards for my friends including those at the British Consulate. Before leaving, I gave them to our driver, Shambhu, to deliver.

The flight was delayed an hour.

As soon as we landed at Bharatpur airport, my eyes went towards the gate. Even though I'd said "Don't come", I had a feeling that someone might be there. Whether it was because I was secretly hoping that someone would come or because I was still not thinking straight, I felt like all the faces I saw were familiar.

There was a lady in a red sari leaning on the airport wall. My eyes went straight to her red sari. I was nervous. Was it my eldest sister? She was always more forceful than me. Once she said something, it was done. Nobody could stop her.

It was her.

I walked slowly towards her with my luggage. Sharada Shah, Gopal Kafle and a few other friends had also come. They looked just like a group of family members waiting outside an operating theatre for news of a patient.

As soon as I got near to them, my sister came and embraced me. She took my face in her hands and cried loudly.

She held me for a long time. She cried for a long time.

It was as if somebody was trying to take me away and she was trying to stop them.

I couldn't hold back my tears after my sister, stronger, taller, chubbier and more forceful than me, started to cry.

I sobbed too.

My body had started to ache but still she kept clinging to me.

I said "So many people have lost their lives. Many of my friends are still in Jumla. I was able to leave and come here now just because of my position. Even if I had died, you would have needed to be strong."

As soon as she heard the word "died", she started to wail. I was also crying and it was embarrassing.

"What are you doing, Sis?" I said. "You're meant to be more mature than I am. What has happened to me? Nothing. So please calm down."

Slowly her wailing stopped although her tears were still flowing. She kept on crying all the way home.

The thought of how my parents might be feeling and how I should comfort them started to make me worried. What if my father's heart couldn't stand the emotional jolt of seeing alive after such a brutal attack? What if my mother was so overcome by emotion that she had an asthma attack? Thoughts like that were going around in my mind.

It was just a coincidence but the driver of the taxi that took us from Bharatpur airport to our home was an old friend of my father. He was a very good friend of my father when they sold milk together. They recognised each other immediately and in all my life I have never seen

Father hug someone so hard. They talked together for quite some time. I was not the focus of my father's attention at all. The fears that I had about how he would react when he saw me faded away. I started talking with the relatives and neighbours who had gathered outside the house. My sister had gone inside by then.

I didn't want to go to my mother immediately. I wanted my sister to talk to my mother first so I stayed outside chatting with the neighbours. I didn't use the main door to enter the house. With many thoughts swirling through my mind, I slowly opened the backdoor and went inside.

I had gone to my mother with so much fear in my heart but inside I found her comforting my sister. Radha Pandey was also there. My sister was continuously sobbing but my mother wasn't crying at all. I thought, I was worried about my mother for nothing. She was, after all, the mother who always taught us "Crying doesn't solve anything."

My mother was calm as she looked at me. I'm sure she felt very sad about what I had been through but there were no tears. Instead, she became very serious and repeatedly said, "You had us very worried."

Father seemed to have missed me more. He stayed by my side until late at night, saying nothing but not leaving me for even one second. He just looked at me and touched me. Maybe he couldn't believe I was alive and wanted to be sure, by touching me.

Secure in his love, I lay down in my warm bed, at home. It was the fifth day after the Jumla attack and I was safe in my own bed. But my soul felt dead.

I took deep breathes and stared at the ceiling. Suddenly, tears began to roll out of the corners of my eyes. I wiped them away but they came again, streaming down my cheeks.

I don't know when I finally dozed off.

Whenever someone opened a door loudly, I felt afraid. Loud voices hurt my ears and I got goose bumps.

For some time in the night, I would sleep deeply but then it would feel like someone was pressing on my throat. My breath stopped and I choked. I immediately woke up. I also had bad dreams. Then I would wake up in a panic, sweating all over.

I must have been showing signs of post-traumatic stress.

I had fear. I didn't want to talk to anybody or eat anything. I didn't want to go out of the house at all. I took medicine and rested.

After staying locked in my home for a week, the Kathmandu office rang me. Susane became very serious and said, "Do you need counselling? If so, we'll arrange it."

I didn't say anything.

Again she asked, "Will you be able to work or not?"

That question hit a nerve. It wounded my self-esteem. If I were in her place, I probably would have asked the same question. But when I was on the receiving end, it hurt my ego. "This is my country," I replied in a stern voice, "The conflict is a problem common to all Nepalis, not just those in Jumla.

Every Nepali should accept this reality. You should accept it. I should accept it. Since I have experienced conflict in a war zone, my mind might not be in the best place right now. I might be stressed. But, even so, I am not unable to work. If the conflict made people unable to work, then the whole country wouldn't be able to work.

She listened silently.

"I also don't need counselling. I am mentally and physically fit. I've spent time with my family. I'm feeling reinvigorated."

I stood up from the chair.

"I will go back to Jumla," I said confidently.

9

JUMLA AGAIN

It was unbearably cold. There was no greenery. The peach trees looked like pine trees -brown and bare. There were no leaves and no fruit. The barren land was all white, covered with snow.

I returned to Jumla in weather like that, in the fourth week after the attack.

"Oh! Radha, you've come back!

The chief of Jumla airport was surprised. Others were also shocked. There was happiness on the faces of Sunil *dai*, Goma *bhauju*, Grandma and the children, as well as concern about my future.

"Jumla is going to ruin your life," Goma *bhauju* always told me.

I said, "*Bhauju*, now Jumla is my life."

Sunil *dai* didn't say anything. He just worried if I didn't come home on time. He still sent the children to look for me before sunset while he strolled towards the bazaar.

Grandma also looked for me from the verandah until I came home.

Their love and support had given me the courage to return to Jumla.

Among our employees affected by the attack, I was the first to come back. Many had thought that our programme had ended but I was not going to let that happen. I was filled with the feeling that I should help heal the wounds of Jumla to the best of my ability.

My state of mind was as stable as Mt Kanjirowa but Jumla was sleeping. After the Maoist attack, neither Jumla nor the Jumlis had recovered.

The scars of the clash were still evident in Khalanga Bazaar. The remains of the burnt buildings were left as they were. Bullet holes in the walls were not patched. The smell of burnt wood was everywhere. The DAO had temporarily moved to the District Development Committee building. There were two or three chairs in a room and they were trying their best to show that the district administration was still running. They were trying to project the image that the district was secure, however, some police were in despair. The administration was not running well. It was not safe. And everybody knew it.

The hospital had closed all its services except emergency. The bank was closed. Some employees from out of the district still hadn't returned. They had stayed in Nepalganj or Surkhet. Most of the government offices had only people acting in the top positions.

Rumours of new attacks by the Maoists made the situation worse. Newcomers to the district were petrified. Most of the old development projects were closed. There were no signs of new projects beginning.

In addition, the attack and the rows of dead bodies the next day had stuck in my mind. I couldn't let go of that memory.

In front of me was a mountain of goals I had set for myself but there was a no way for me to climb up and there was no-one to help me. How could I make that climb? Without a calm mind, how could I move forward without falling? And, in any case, could my individual efforts bring about any change in Jumla?

These questions came to my mind again and again. I was daunted by the challenge I was facing, and facing it alone. But I was also not ready to give up.

I had to climb that mountain by any means. If I left without building an operating theatre and blood transfusion unit in the Jumla hospital, I might be able to face my parents but how could I face myself?

The more I thought about it, the more confident I became.

When I first came to Jumla, the death of a pregnant lady deeply disturbed me. I was unable to save that lady who had been brought to the hospital after excessive bleeding due to a retained placenta. From that time on, I had promised myself I would build an operating theatre and blood bank and create an emergency fund for the Jumla hospital.

While the Safe Motherhood Programme was in place and construction of the new hospital buildings, including the operating theatre, was continuing, I was moving forward towards fulfilling my dreams. Back in Jumla, I realised that I had to pick up where I'd left off.

I had realised some time earlier that foreign-financed aid projects were not making Jumla self-sufficient but, instead, more dependent. Many important foreign researchers also came to Jumla, got what they wanted and left without giving anything back. Many social workers who had used Jumla as a rung on the ladder of their careers, forgot all about the place once they got to the top. I wanted to put a stop to all these things.

In June 2004, the new hospital building and operating theatre were completed and the Safe Motherhood Programme ended. But I had left the job before that and was fully devoted to my own cause which was mustering the resources to build a delivery suite and a blood transfusion service, as well as providing support for the emergency department.

I went from the District Administration to the District Development Committee looking for contributions and also involved the local community. I asked for help from political leaders, the police and the army.

I asked everyone to support the cause of their own free will. Some gave the equivalent of the cost of a day's lunch and some even gave their salary for a day. The police and army gave lump sums. But still it was not enough, so a system was set up at Jumla airport whereby all passengers going from Jumla had to contribute Rs 10. We collected the money as the passengers were boarding. In this way, we collected Rs 350,000 for blood transfusion services and Rs 650,000 for the emergency relief fund.

The emergency relief fund was established to help the patients who had to be taken to Nepalganj or Surkhet for treatment which was unavailable in Jumla. It would be given on the basis of economic need. I had seen numerous cases where people lost their lives just because they didn't have enough money to go for a check-up outside of Jumla.

What could be more terrible than to lose a life simply because someone couldn't afford to access health services? With the relief fund in place, no poor person would ever have to face that situation again. At first, Safe Motherhood had said that they would provide the seed money. When they hesitated, I got into a heated discussion with them and eventually they gave Rs 150,000.

As a result of everyone's combined efforts, we were able to perform four major operations in 2003-2004. All four of them were related to childbirth, including a dangerous breach birth and a case of serious bleeding. We were able to do C-sections and save both the children and the mothers.

Nobody had expected that operations like that would ever be possible in Jumla hospital. Previously there had been no alternative but to take the patients to Nepalganj or Surkhet.

Today the face of Jumla hospital has completely changed. It's no longer just a district hospital but has been transformed into the Karnali Academy of Health Sciences and Teaching. General operations of all sorts are being performed there. The hospital has been successful in performing operations relating to appendicitis and even orthopaedics.

Two or three operations relating to pregnancy are performed every month. There is no longer a lack of doctors, nurses or other health professionals. After the Academy was created, it got more funding and additional doctors as well.

Looking at all this, I feel satisfied. This was the result of a collaborative effort. It was not something that could be achieved single-handed. I was afraid that I wouldn't be able to achieve my goals. But I took the first step up and then others joined me climbing the mountain.

After the success of this initiative, I became even more involved with Jumla. Apart from health services, I started to get involved in other activities to benefit society, such as educating and training orphans and poor children.

Then I decided to do something else.

I went to the DAO and said, "Let's celebrate Kartik 29, the day after the Maoist attack as 'Peace Day'. On that day, let's organise a programme to remember all the known and unknown people who died in that attack. It will send a message of reconciliation and help inspire everyone to get involved in the development of Jumla."

I had expected this proposal to be easily accepted because it related to Jumla's development and imagined I would be organising the first programme on Kartik 29, 2060 (15 November 2003).

But I was not successful.

Everyone bit their tongues when they heard my proposal. All the office chiefs including the Chief District Officer were new. They had heard about the frightful events in Jumla but hadn't experienced them. To them, it was just an incident that they had heard about and, therefore, they were unmoved. Moreover, the conflict in the country still wasn't over. Nobody wanted to risk antagonising either the Maoists or the security forces.

But I was not going to give up.

I contacted Jumlis who had moved to Surkhet, Nepalganj and Kathmandu and asked them to support the idea. We started in Kathmandu with a small programme remembering Kartik 29. Later, we decided to create and register an organisation and start working in a formal way.

As a result of this, "Action Works Nepal" was established in 2010 and that same year we were able to organise a programme successfully in Jumla. We have organised events annually since then.

From this organisation, we have started an initiative called "Miteri Village - Let's Live Together".

The main objective of the Miteri Village initiative is to heal the wounds caused by 10 years of conflict. To do this, we focus on raising awareness at the local level.

We provide extra part-time teachers as needed to improve education in Jumla schools. We also train permanent teachers and provide scholarships to the needy. By 2012 our programmes were running in 30 schools in Jumla and Kalikot. We are planning to expand our activities into Humla and Achham.

There are some humanitarian aid programmes as well. In May 2011, a child was weeding corn fields. A bomb blew up in the field damaging both his eyes. We paid for his treatment in Kathmandu for a year as well as surgery. Now he is able to see. Efforts are also focused on rehabilitating people affected by the conflict by training them in income generating skills.

Our organisation is also helping in cases, including litigation, related to domestic violence and sexual abuse of women. At first we file a case at the local level. If justice is not done then we take the case to Kathmandu. We are also raising voices on promoting women's rights at the national level. We are fighting for the eradication of the *chhaupadi* tradition which is prevalent in western Nepal. According to this tradition, women who are menstruating are considered unclean and must leave the house to stay in the cowshed. We are also lobbying for meaningful representation of women in politics.

Our funding for these activities comes from many sources, including various national and international organisations and as well as individuals. In 2012, we were able to collect USD 10,000. In the first four months of 2013 alone, we collected Rs 900,000. I, myself, am working as a volunteer in this organisation. My personal expenses are being taken care of by my father and my younger sister, Samjhana.

I first came to Jumla as an employee of an international aid programme. The programme ended but my work there did not. I stayed in Jumla. I became Jumli. I never expected any sort of recognition for my efforts and I still don't, but in 2012 I received two awards in the same year.

For my work in a conflict-affected zone, the University of San Diego, USA, awarded me with "Woman Peace-Maker 2012" and the United Nations Development Programme gave me the "N-Peace Award 2012", an award for women building peace in Asia.

Whether I was qualified or not, I'm not sure. But one thing is for sure: these two awards have raised my confidence. I have again started to dream big.

And my steps have become stronger than ever.

Mahashankar Devkota, the father of Bhanu who survived with me under the same roof during the Maoist attack, considers me a goddaughter and has given me 1.5 ropanis of land in Jumla.

"My son and this lady came back from death's door together," he said while transferring the title of the land to me, "She is my goddaughter."

The land is in Bohoragaun, just over the suspension bridge across the Tila River. I have announced that I will build the Miteri Peace Garden there. I have a plan to establish a monument in memory of all the people who died during the attack. I am also thinking of creating a meditation and yoga centre.

I always say, a person's birthplace is not his choice. Some are born into rich families in rich countries and become rich through no effort of their own. Some are born into poor families in poor countries.

This is no-one's choice. Wherever we are born, wherever we are raised, we can all live together. We have the capacity in us to share our resources with those less fortunate than ourselves and to lift their economic status. The only question is how we decide to go about it.

"Miteri Village - Let's live together" is an effort to find an answer to that question.

AND, FINALLY…

As a child, I always worried that my mother might go to hell.

I overheard a priest in the village saying to my mother, "Gangamaya, you don't have a son. Maybe you will go to hell."

I didn't know what hell really was. I just knew it was full of horrors. People were fried in oil and their skin was stripped off. Salt and pepper was then rubbed on their bodies. They were hanged upside down and whipped. They were not given any food or clothes. Monsters tortured them every day and every night.

That's why my heart sank when I heard the priest say that to my mother.

Later I understood that all the mothers in the village who didn't have a son felt cursed. People said, "They can only cross the Vaitarani River if a son lights their funeral pyre."

My mother didn't go to visit most of the neighbours to avoid hearing such evil things. She also didn't visit her mother's home that often. She became very angry inside but didn't say anything out loud.

By coincidence, she gave birth to a son after us, five sisters.

I was happy that I had a brother now. I was happy that my mother didn't have to go to hell.

Now my mother would be able to also cross the Vaitarani.

I have inherited traits from both my parents.

My father taught me to dream and my mother gave me the courage to pursue my dreams without a faint heart.

I have never met any woman to match my mother's strong character and I'm not saying that just because she was my mother. Her attitude was such that it was hard to believe that she was an uneducated village woman.

She was extremely interested in reading and writing. During childhood, my maternal uncles used to study sitting under the trees but Mother wasn't allowed to join them. She hid and looked at them from afar. "Sometimes I used to hear your uncles reading, sometimes I couldn't hear," said Mother, "You have a chance to read and write. You are lucky. Don't miss the chance."

The buffer zone around the Chitwan National Park was a 10 minute walk from our home. At that time, it was allowed to cut grass and collect firewood in the zone. I used to take classes in the morning. After returning from school at eleven, I used to go to the jungle with my mother to take the buffaloes to graze. This was our daily routine.

There were lots of pine trees in the jungle. Pine cones fell onto the ground as thickly as stars in the sky. We collected and burned them so that only the seeds remained. We collected those seeds and took them to the bazaar to sell. At that time I didn't know why pine seeds could be sold. I thought people make soap from them. I just understood that the cash that came from selling those seeds helped somewhat with our family expenses. It helped to buy some medicines for my mother.

Whenever we went to the bazaar to sell the seeds, Mother always talked to me about studying. "We work so hard all day and, in the end, I don't even know how much I earned," she said. "You shouldn't become like me. Study hard."

My mother, who always complained about not being able to go to school and get educated, later joined adult literacy classes. At an old age, she learned the alphabet and to write her own name.

I have learned not to leave my dreams unfulfilled and to pursue those dreams by any means possible. I learned that from my mother.

Our home and our farm were ten minutes' walk away from each other. One day, my mother and I were going to the farm to add composted cow manure. As we were coming back, we came across a dead body in a culvert. The smell was so bad that I couldn't stand it and held my nose.

"Why are you holding your nose?" scolded my mother.

"It smells really bad," I replied.

"This is a body, just like ours," she said. "If you die after doing good, then people will take you to Devghat, otherwise you will lie dead just like this person. We shouldn't feel repulsed. We should learn from seeing this."

"What is there to learn from a dead body?" I asked, not understanding what she was talking about.

"This happens if you live your life like a dog. Whether you

want to live like a dog or like a human is in your hands."

I learned from my mother to look at life compassionately and with a wide perspective.

We had a neighbour, a rich man. They had a very big farm. Their daughter-in-law once said to my mother, "When will the work in the fields ever end? I get so tired."

Mother scolded her. "How lazy are you! You shouldn't ask when your work will be finished. Work is the foundation stone of our lives. And we have to work in somebody else's field. At least you have your own farm to work on. And you are complaining instead of being happy?"

I have inherited my work ethic from my mother.

I never saw my mother healthy and fit. She had asthma from the time I can remember. She started breathing heavily after only a little exertion. She coughed all night long. Once she started, she coughed so loudly for 15 or 20 minutes that I felt her lungs would come out. Many times we had to rush her to hospital, thinking she was going to die.

She used to go to bed as soon as dinner was over. She left the washing up until the morning. During childhood, I thought Mother was doing that just because she wanted to. I only understood after I became a nurse. After dinner, when her full stomach pressed on her lungs, the oxygen flow would be reduced but Mother didn't want to show her pain to others. She would just said, "I feel very sleepy after eating rice. I can't work at all."

Sometimes, when guests came, she couldn't go to bed without talking with them. So she used to feed everyone else, talk with them and only eat her own dinner after the guests had gone to bed. Her body was getting very lean and thin. We were unable to take her for regular check-ups due to lack of money. But, still, I didn't see her worried or frightened. She fought with disease and poverty all her life but I never saw her shed a tear. Sometimes if we sisters made unhappy faces and cried, she told us, "Crying is not the solution to anything."

Whatever woes there might be in life, I had learned not to lose courage and to remain strong.

My mother was a thousand times more progressive than many feminists today. Our relatives and society in general considered her cursed for not having a son. The day she had a son, everybody's mouths were silenced, even those who had bad-mouthed her in the past. But my mother used to muse about different matters. She wanted to challenge society and its tradition of treating sons and daughters differently. She said to me, "Radha, after I die, you five sisters light my funeral pyre. I want to cross the Vaitarani from fire given by my daughters."

I got goose bumps.

But what should I answer? I couldn't say anything.

Seeing me silent, she repeated the same thing again and again until I said "Yes".

Then she said, "Don't cover my head with anything while carrying my dead body. I want to go to Devghat with a bare head, so that everyone can see my face for the last time. All my life I have lived in pain. I don't want to be suffocated. I feel uneasy even when I see other people being tied up."

This was also against tradition I couldn't do anything but respect my mother's wishes. I said okay.

Finally she said, "None of you have to carry out the mourning rituals for me. Instead, use that money so that poor children will be able to read."

I accepted that as well.

There are many people who shout slogans such as "We shouldn't follow bad traditions!" But there are very few people who actually stop following those bad traditions. People have to be courageous then we can cross mountains that no-one ever dreamed of conquering. Even if it's a tradition which has existed for generations, if it's a bad tradition then we must let it go. I learned that lesson from my mother.

Today I am already 40. I am living my life in accordance with to my ideals, my beliefs and my determination. I dream just like my father taught me and I pursue my dreams just like my mom said. They never interfered in my life nor did they ever put obstacles in my path, so much so that my mother didn't even worry whether I was going to marry or not. When someone asked her "Won't your daughter marry?", she replied, "Marriage is a personal choice. We shouldn't pressure anyone."

I don't know why but despite this she used to tell my youngest sister to get married. One day she astonished us. She was seriously affected by asthma and we were giving her oxygen at home. My youngest sister was also there and Mother grabbed her hand and said, "You get married, Okay?"

My sister didn't say anything because this wasn't the first time my mother had said this to her but on this occasion my mother was very persistent, saying over and over "Just tell me now. Will you do what I say or not?"

Eventually, my sister said, "Yes, Mother. I'll do it."

Then my mother took a deep breath.

Then she didn't breathe again. That was the New Year's Day of 2066 (14 April 2009).

The sun had just started to rise. But the sun in my life had just set.

I started working on the last rites for my mother. My older sisters, Binu and Usha, my younger sister, Samjhana, and my brother, Kishor, were together. Bindu, my other sister, was not there, however, because her father-in-law had died only two days earlier.

We wrapped Mother's body and laid it, unbound, on a stretcher with her head uncovered.

The priest doing the last rites objected but I was determined to fulfil my mother's final wishes at any cost.

We rented a van to transport my mother's body and the mourners. Usually mourners need to walk to the river. My mother's wish was to spare them that pain.

We reached Devghat.

It was time to offer holy water to the soul and to set fire to the pyre.

According to my mother's wish, I stepped forward. Our priest didn't like the idea of a daughter lighting the fire, especially when a son was present. He became adamant that it should be done according to tradition.

"Your brother should light the pyre," he said, "That is what the religious texts say."

"I don't know what the texts say, *baje*," I said, "But this is what my mother wanted."

After arguing for about an hour, the priest agreed on a compromise. "I will not stop you doing it if your father agrees."

Now the final decision rested with my father.

Father came near to the priest. He bowed his head and held both hands together. "Son or daughter?" he said, "For me, both are equal."

I gave *mukhaagni* to my mother with my own hands and lit her funeral pyre.

All her last wishes were fulfilled.

I don't know the difference between heaven and hell. I just believe this: after death the soul goes to neither heaven nor hell. It just stays here among the people who were its loved ones.

The soul is in heaven when those it loves are happy. And their pain is its hell.

My mother is always here. Among us. With me.

Therefore, I always want to remain content. I know my mother's heaven is in my happiness.

In the name of my parents, before the death of my mother we established the Ganga-Devi scholarship fund. It selects socially outcast students, *dalits*, who have failed their exams and gives them a scholarship – a second chance.

My younger sister also married two years ago.

The only thing I regret is that I couldn't share my mother's pain. Mother used to cough day and night and had trouble breathing. I went to Jumla and stayed there for my own vocation. Mother used to say, "Can't you work and stay in Chitwan?'

At the time, I took it lightly. Now I think, did my mother want her nurse daughter to be with her when she couldn't bear the pain? If that is true, then not understanding what she wanted must be the biggest mistake of my life.

Six months before her death, I found out she had lung cancer. I haven't said this to my father even now. The last six months of her life were really painful for her. I know that it's very difficult to live with externally provided oxygen for six months. I don't think I could have done anything for my mother even after becoming a nurse but I regret not trying.

Father is 77. He stays in Chitwan with my brother's family. His body is still strong. He can work on the farm though he needs to take some medication. He has started to feel a bit lonely after Mother's death. So he comes to see me quite often. We also talk on the phone a lot. My other sisters also care for him.

I took my father to Jumla in 2012. It was the first time he'd been there in 52 years though many times when I visited home he'd told me he wanted to go back there with me.

"This is a time of conflict," I said, "We can go later."

The day when I said "Let's go to Jumla", my father was elated.

Father had come to Jumla in 1960 on foot, staying overnight in different places. He doesn't remember how many days it took him to get there. He had gone by way of Jajarkot. While returning, he went via Kalikot, Dailekh, and Doti.

We were, however, flying on a plane with Sita Airways.

As soon as he stepped into Khalanga Bazaar he said

cheerfully, "Jumla has totally changed! The bazaar is so big."

During his four-day stay in Jumla, he roamed around like a child. He tried to find a lot of places he knew from the old days but he couldn't locate them.

The only things he recognised were the tap and the big tree and the Chandannath and Bhairavnath temples. He became emotional when he came to the Tila River. He put his hands in the water and, lost in his old memories, said nothing for a long time.

The office of *Anchalaadhis* used to be where the Everest Hotel was, he recalled. Now the Everest Hotel is also not there anymore. Sunil *dai* has moved to Surkhet. When I am on the way to Jumla, I go to see them. Our relationship is still strong.

Father was very happy when he was strolling around Khalanga Bazaar but he became sad when he started to move around the village.

The sad, naked children he remembered. Cracked hands and legs due to cold. Hair never washed and matted. Running noses. Dried mucus on lips and cheeks. Old houses. Trash and flies everywhere. Women not knowing how to express themselves and, even if they knew how, being hesitant to do so in front of strangers.

"I thought Jumla had changed," he said ,"But only a small part has changed. Village life is still the same. Lodging, food, and clothing - nothing has changed."

Father became sad after seeing that so little in Jumla had changed in five decades.

He said, "Chitwan has become so much more prosperous

but Jumla is still the same. From the time I was last here till now, what have the people here been doing?"

I didn't have the answer to his question.

Those who are accountable have kept mum. Or has anybody even asked them?

Why hadn't Jumla changed?

One of the things my father said made me cheerful though.

He said, "Jumla is still poorer than us. Your service to Jumla hasn't finished yet."

13 YEARS LATER

25 April 2015. It was a sunny morning in Khalanga and I was meeting the Chief District Officer of Jumla, Dipendra Raj Paudel, for brunch. He had invited me to his quarters at the District Administration Office. Roshana Kandel was also there.

As we discussed events following the Maoist attack on Khalanga 13 years earlier, including the establishment of the Miteri Peace Learning Centre, something strange happened. At first I thought a passing tractor was making the building shake but then I realised we were experiencing an earthquake. A small earthquake had shaken Khalanga three days earlier so initially I said nothing.

The others also felt it and it was a quite a shake. Roshana started crying while other people ran around looking for cover. Seeing the others panicking, I laughed and told them to calm down and not overreact.

The earthquake really didn't affect Khalanga very much. I thought it was just another tremor. Later, when reports of devastation started coming in from Kathmandu and other places, I was shocked. I had come to Jumla from Kathmandu only a few days earlier. I was worried about the Action Works Nepal (AWON) family.

A special meeting was scheduled at the AWON office in Kathmandu that day as Popular Gentle, AWON's Vice President, had also arrived. For 24 hours the mobile phone network was dead so I had no way of knowing if people I knew in Kathmandu were all right.

This was a very stressful time.

People, including Roshana, were trying to contact their friends and relatives in Kathmandu using satellite phones. For me, the whole experience brought back the trauma of the Khalanga attack and its aftermath.

The following day, I managed to call my brother-in-law, Umakanta Regmi, in Chitwan. "All are safe in Kathmandu," he said.

As soon as I heard those words, I breathed a huge sigh of relief.

After the mobile network and internet services were restored, I was flabbergasted to see texts, emails and Facebook messages flooding in, inquiring about my whereabouts. Friends and acquaintances living abroad expressed their concern about the massive loss of life and property in Nepal. This reminded me of AWON's underlying philosophy: *Miteri*, a concept of mutual love and respect beyond the ties of blood and marriage. I became emotional.

With tears rolling down my cheeks, I decided I had to do something for the people affected by this earthquake.

I immediately wrote a post on Facebook, urging people to help me raise funds for relief work.

Fortunately, I could communicate with Laxmi Pandey, a staffer at AWON. I asked Pandey to contact Gentle to get the relief work started. How could I stay in Jumla? With the help of Police Inspector Prem Bahadur Khadka in Jumla and travel agent Bishnu Rawat in Nepalganj, I flew to Kathmandu on 28 April.

As soon as I arrived I went to the Tribhuvan University Teaching Hospital in Maharajganj to volunteer, along with five nurses. We also donated 10 sphygmomanometers.

The government had given permission for AWON to go to Bhandarithok of Sitapokhari VDC in Sindhupalchok to carry out relief work there but I couldn't leave Kathmandu immediately because there was no vehicle available to take. On 29 April, the acquaintance of a friend provided a four-wheel-drive for a week to help us with our mission.

It was decided AWON would target its efforts on remote areas. We worked in the nine districts which had been worst affected by the earthquake.

We focused on relief distribution and residential medical camps, paying special attention to pregnant women, lactating mothers, children under five, adolescent girls, widows, *dalits*, elderly people and bereaved families. Besides food and materials like tarpaulins, mats and ropes, we distributed white clothing to the families who were in mourning and sanitary items to teenage girls.

At least 12,000 families in the nine districts benefitted from our support.

On the second week we ran out of funds. I made another appeal on Facebook and sent emails to my contacts abroad asking for support.

Gradually, we started receiving donations.

One of our groups was running a medical camp at Bankhuchaur in Kavrepalanchok when the second big hit the region on 12 May.

There were no government agencies or INGOs operating there. I went to Dolakha alone. On the way, I saw 150 landslides from the highway.

I worked for up to 20 hours a day for 45 days.

The 2015 earthquakes exposed how inadequate, if not inefficient, the government and key INGOs' disaster preparedness really was. Witnessing the devastation caused by the two big earthquakes and the resulting humanitarian crisis in central and eastern Nepal, I couldn't stop myself from imagining what would happen in the remote areas of mid-western and far-western Nepal in case of a natural disaster.

Experts say big earthquakes are due in the western Nepal since 1505 owing to the stress that has built up for hundreds of years.

In the wake of the earthquakes, I feared the shift of the focus of development and reconstruction from Karnali and western Nepal to the east, which had started in 2009 after the Maoists came to the peace process, would only get worse. The border blockade imposed by India from September 2015 to February 2016 paralysed Nepal's economy and created another unprecedented crisis across the country.

The Karnali region, which had been left high and dry due to government neglect, was deeply affected. But the woes of Karnali were under-reported as usual, as if ignoring the region had become normal behaviour.

Seeing impoverished children in Jumla, I always recall my own childhood.

I used to go to school bare foot and plant paddy in other people's fields for minimal wage. Many times I had to skip dinner as my parents didn't have enough to feed us all. I used to think it was only my family who lived like that until, at the age of 27, I came to Jumla and realised that wasn't true. The two *dalit* boys whom I met as soon as my plane touched down in Jumla really opened my eyes.

After surviving the Khalanga attack in 2002, I was searching for an answer as to why it was that I had emerged unharmed while many others didn't. As a result, I made a commitment to do something significant for Jumla and its people.

A vibrant trade hub in ancient times, Karnali has been left neglected and impoverished. The Kathmandu-based policy-makers and INGOs seem to be ignorant of, if not indifferent towards, the real issues affecting Jumla and the entire Karnali region.

Giving up a well-paid job, I had decided to serve in Karnali. My passion and commitment to do something for Karnali and its hard-working people guided me to make that decision, which many considered foolish.

I have dedicated my life to Karnali and am doing whatever I can both at a personal level and through AWON, which is a charity I founded with like-minded friends. In fact, our aim through Miteri Village is a global campaign for peace and justice but for legal reasons we have to be registered as a local NGO.

AWON works to empower poor, vulnerable and socially

excluded people so they may live with justice and equality. Our objective is to improve the livelihood of communities through innovative humanitarian, educational, and vocational result-driven programmes around political, economic, social, cultural and environmental empowerment, moving forward to peace, growth and sustainable development.

I have been a vocal critic of the modus operandi of most NGOs and INGOs. They lobby and bring in funds, which they spend largely on administrative costs. They sponsor overseas trips for government officials and influence them for their own benefit which has promoted poor governance and corruption. It's no secret that NGOs and INGOs have done little to remove economic and class inequities and in some instances have actually made them worse.

I recall how I started my own NGO. I had met Dr. Durga Pokharel, the first chairperson of the National Women's Commission, in Jumla. After many conversations with her, mostly over the telephone, I started believing that I could do something on my own.

In 2004, I spent nine months in Kathmandu. I stayed at my friend Binita Paudel's house in Arubari. During my time there, I tried to build up connections with potential supporters. I took part in different public programmes as well as many workshops, seminars and, at times, confidential meetings behind closed doors with the help of Dr. Pokharel. When I spoke, people wanted to know more about Jumla, especially the security situation there in the wake of the Maoist attack, and they called me a "brave lady".

I met many ministers, activists, social workers, businesswomen, artists, politicians and people from different walks of life. Most of them seemed excited to hear about my work in Jumla and expressed their readiness to support me but when I actually approached them for support, they cold-shouldered me.

I had already realised I wouldn't fit into the government structure. I had to work either as a lone wolf or together with like-minded people. I was looking for a proper platform. In the meantime, my sister Samjhana founded an NGO in Chitwan which I joined as a volunteer even though I was working in Jumla. But that NGO didn't last long due to lack of funds and disharmony among the board members. Later, I came to be in touch with professors and PhDs from the Rampur-based Institute of Agriculture. They had formed a group called Madhuban that would invest in agriculture. I borrowed Rs 50,000 to put into the venture, without letting my family know. I trusted the board members blindly but later discovered that nepotism and corruption were rampant in Madhuban.

What I got in return for my Rs 50,000 was a meagre two kilograms of beans and breach of trust. Newly appointed board members went abroad taking advantage of my name and the venture was eventually closed. Later, my sister Samjhana invested some money in a Pokhara-based community hospital on my behalf. But we lost all the money.

After the completion of her tenure in the National Women's Commission, Dr. Pokharel was making preparations to start a new NGO. She asked me to join the board as an executive member. I agreed, despite knowing little about the NGO. But the founders – Uma Karki and Dr. Pokharel herself– went to the US one after the other and the NGO couldn't do anything substantial – just hold meetings.

I came across other people who also showed an interest in Karnali but would do nothing meaningful. I was frustrated.

After nine months in Kathmandu, I started exploring job opportunities. I briefly worked for Plan International outside Kathmandu and then joined CEDPA. Later, I also worked for CARE Nepal. I felt, however, that these INGOs didn't want to go outside their comfort zones. There were also cliques and discrimination among the staff.

This vexed me further and I decided to quit. I went to the Philippines for a course, sponsored by the Asian Development Bank, which aimed at generating leaders to work in the field of poverty alleviation in Asia. It helped me build up my confidence besides garnering various skills. There I realised that what I was trying to do in Nepal was advocacy and fund-raising for social causes.

After meeting the two *dalit* boys in Jumla, I had started focusing on the fact that an individual's birth place is not a matter of choice. After finishing the course, I considered working in Africa, however, my friends – Bharat Wasti, Binita Paudel and Popular Gentle – told me they were not happy with the ongoing development discourse and wanted to start a new organisation.

This led to the founding of Action Works Nepal in 2010. Samjhana and Saroj Dahal also agreed to come on board.

AWON took me back to Jumla for good. We decided that AWON would focus on training, research, health, education, entrepreneurship and livelihood, as well as climate change, peace building and human rights, in order to overcome poverty and cultivate the culture of peace. "Miteri Gaun-Let's Live Together" is its lead strategy.

Miteri is an indigenous cultural concept based on the idea of establishing friendly relationships, above those of blood or marriage, between individuals regardless of their region, religion, gender, class, caste or creed. Traditionally, *miteri* was limited to relationships between individuals but seeing its tremendous potential in relation to community mediation, community harmony and cohesion, peace building and bringing positive changes in society through recognition of cultural diversity, equality and justice, we took up this ancient concept as our strategy.

"Miteri Gaun – Let's Live Together" encompasses policies, strategies and actions to ensure organisation, and reflects intercultural dialogue, understanding and cooperation in a practical way in conflict-affected, remote, poor and marginalised areas. It possesses a combination of characteristics including organisational policies, training and critical monitoring. What's more, it mobilises local people.

During my visits to far-flung districts, I see that places, other than district headquarters, haven't changed much in the past decade. Though the Maoist rebels laid down their arms and joined the political mainstream, development and reconstruction have not happened.

I believe absence of war does not constitute peace when so many social maladies remain and so many people struggle daily to live a hand-to-mouth existence.

People are still bare-foot and ill-clad in remote villages. They have to depend on the sun or firewood to warm them when their hamlets are knee-deep in snow. We started the Miteri Recycling Centre, which collects used clothing in Kathmandu, recycles it and then sells it to the needy at minimal cost. This venture was inspired by the model of social business put forward by Nobel Laureate Prof Muhammad Yunus of Bangladesh.

There are health facilities in all Village Development Committees (VDCs) and, according to the rules, birthing centres are supposed to operate around the clock. But pregnant and lactating women are still dying for want of proper treatment. There are policies, structures and, at least theoretically, human resources, and yet there are no services. Most of the people posted to government health facilities don't even show up for duty. Many others are affiliated with political parties or trade unions and take advantage of their connections to avoid going to remote places. And yet no one is held accountable or punished for dereliction of duty.

Seeing the high maternal mortality rate in Sannigaun, we set up a birthing centre there. This facility provides service 24 hours every day.

Now women come to the birthing centre rather than going to the cowshed, where they would traditionally deliver their babies without any assistance. We have sponsored two local girls who are pursuing staff nurse and ANM courses and who will hopefully take over the running of the project.

We collected funds for the birthing centre through the concept of Miteri. Local residents donated labour to build two rooms with an attached bathroom, while the Non-Resident Nepali Association's UK chapter launched a Miteri campaign to collect funds for the five-year project. Most of the donors are nurses.

The Miteri Birthing Centre at Sannigaun is just a start. We plan to expand and build birthing centres in other villages too.

There are schools but many children don't attend. People are yet to understand the importance of education. Many children enrol but the rate of absenteeism and dropping out is very high. Parents have limited sources of income and send their children to collect fodder or work in the fields as agricultural labourers instead of sending them to school. Even teachers are not qualified and schools lack proper infrastructure. Primary schools running five classes in two rooms is a common sight. Many sixth graders can't even write their names in the Roman script even though English is a compulsory subject from the beginning of primary school. School management committees are also highly politicised.

We have launched the Miteri Education Support Programme with the hope of bringing change to children's education and schools. This programme supports teachers, provides partial or full scholarships to children, helps schools repair or maintain their infrastructure, constructs toilets and distributes sanitary pads to girls and medical kits to others. Also, we help school management committees to provide capacity building training to teachers.

Karnali region is considered the birthplace of the "Nepali" civilisation. It is believed that the Nepali language evolved and spread from there. People still practice some ancient and indigenous ways of peace building and maintaining harmony. People barter goods and engage in cultural events, such as singing and dancing to folk songs and indigenous instruments. People of different castes live in harmony and inter-caste marriage is not rare.

But academic anthropological study of Karnali culture is not enough. We have planned the Miteri Peace Learning

Centre to facilitate research for practical purposes on the culture of Karnali and the surrounding regions.

I donated the royalties of the Nepali version of "Khalanga ma Hamala" to construct the Peace Monument in Jumla. The monument has a message urging global peace and justice inscribed in four languages: the local Jumli dialect, Nepali, English and German. It welcomes visitors to the Miteri Peace Garden which commemorates the people who lost their lives or suffered during the decade-long conflict in Nepal. Members of the local communities built it under the guidance of Austrian sculptor Helga Palassar and her son Michael. It was inaugurated in 2014 on International Peace Day, 21 September.

I have donated a total of Rs 300,000, including the Rs 200,000 I received as part of the Madan Puraskar literary award for "Khalanga ma Hamala", to set up the Miteri Ganga Devi Peace Award, named after my parents.

Four local heroes, who contributed to bringing change to society and to building peace, were honoured with this award in 2015, the first year it was awarded.

Along with AWON I am engaged in the prevention of and response to gender-based violence at the local, national and international level. We were the first organisation to study and speak out against the sexual harassment and abuse of women on public transport in Nepal. We also raised our voices and filed a case of sexual harassment in one highly-reputed university.

We have been part of the Gender Responsive Constitution Building Campaign, Stop Rape Campaign, 100 Days Violence Against Women Campaign and Equal Citizenship Rights

Campaign among others. We have worked on promoting the role of women in peace building and political participation through campaigns associated with UNSCR 1325 and1820 and many educational programmes on gender, inclusion and democracy.

More importantly, AWON has engaged with boys and men to raise awareness of gender equality and the prevention of gender-based violence.

I have always been distressed by the taboos associated with menstruation, seeing the hardships and restrictions imposed upon women when they have their periods. I have been a vocal opponent of these inhuman practices which even to this day still prevail in the Karnali region.

Women are forced to live in *chhaupadi* for 60 days a year, on average, in very sorry conditions. From puberty until menopause women spend almost six years in restricted circumstances. Men also spend over two years in such circumstances along with their mothers during their childhoods.

This restriction is a form of psycho-social suppression which prevents women from accessing opportunities and imposes additional and needless physical suffering on them. It is a key barrier to women's empowerment and to sustainable development and the promotion of peace and human rights in society.

With an aim to end this practice, we have launched a set of activities such as educational programmes for men, women, traditional healers and political leaders, and training, research and media mobilisation at local, national and global levels.

AWON volunteers recently made a documentary on

chhaupadi highlighting the plight of menstruating women. This documentary was shown at the World Feminist and World Rights Film Festivals in the United Kingdom in 2014 and many other forums.

Life expectancy at birth in the Karnali region is far below the national average. Statistics show that people in Karnali are dying a full 18 years earlier than those living in other parts of Nepal. This, I believe, is akin to genocide perpetrated by the state.

Notwithstanding social and economic challenges, Karnali has natural resources and tremendous potential for prosperity but it has been left to atrophy due to the apathy of both state and non-state players.

It's high time we did something substantial to explore this potential and develop the region, though clearly we cannot rely on the government to fulfil that role.

One's place of birth is not a matter of choice. I was born far away from Jumla but went to work there and fell in love with the place and the people.

I started my professional career as an anaesthetic nurse in 1994, working during the peak of the bloody conflict, and I continue to serve as a volunteer in case of emergencies.

I went to the field to serve after the earthquake in 2015, during the border blockade the same year and after the floods in 2016.

I have worn recycled clothes and lived the same life as 90 per cent of the population. Seeing the hardship experienced in daily life by ordinary people, I am committed to do something significant to help them.

But I can't do it all alone; others have to help me.

Those who can extend their hands to me in the spirit of *miteri*, please feel free to make contact.

Thank you.

Radha Paudel

rpaudel456@gmail.com

www.actionworksnepal.com